COASTAL
SUFFOLK

───── ROBERT SIMPER ─────

COASTAL SUFFOLK

Published by Creekside Publishing 2009
www.creeksidepublishing.co.uk

ISBN 978-0-9563299-0-5
COPYRIGHT Robert Simper

Printed by The Lavenham Press

Front Cover: The Barge *Ena* off the Deben Bar
Frontispiece: The Town Steps, Aldeburgh
Back Cover: The Southwold Lighthouse

Books by the same author:

EAST ANGLIAN BOOKS
Over Snape Bridge (1967)
Woodbridge & Beyond (1972)
Suffolk Show (1981)
East Anglian Coast & Waterways (1985)
Suffolk Sandlings (1986)
Woodbridge: Pictorial History (1995)
Suffolk: A Fine Farming County (2007)
Woodbridge to the Coast (2008)

SAIL BOOKS
East Coast Sail (1972)
Scottish Sail (1974)
North East Sail (1975)
British Sail (1977)
Victorian & Edwardian Yachting from Old Photographs (1978)
Gaff Sail (1979)
Sail on the Orwell (1982)
Sail: The Surviving Tradition (1984)

BRITISH ISLES
Britain's Maritime Heritage (1982)
Beach Boats of Britain (1984)

ENGLISH ESTUARIES SERIES
The River Deben (1992)
The River Orwell and the River Stour (1993)
Rivers Alde, Ore and Blyth (1994)
Essex Rivers and Creeks (1995)
Norfolk Rivers and Harbours (1996)
Thames Tideway (1997)
River Medway and The Swale (1998)
Rivers to the Fens (2000)
Up the River Deben (2006)

AUTOBIOGRAPHICAL
In Search of Sail (1998)
Family Fields (1999)
Voyage Around East Anglia (2001)
Creekside Tales (2004)

COAST IN THE PAST SERIES
Forgotten Coast (2002)   British Isles
Sunrise Coast (2002)   Suffolk & N.Essex
The Lugger Coast (2003) Cornwall & Devon
The Barge Coast of Suffolk, Essex and Kent (2007)

CONTENTS

MAP OF COASTAL SUFFOLK

Somerleyton

Ashby

Barnby

Lowestoft

Kessingland

Shadingfield

Benacre

Easton Broad

Wangford

Covehithe

Halesworth

Bulcamp

Blythburgh

Southwold

Walberswick

Dunwich

Westleton

Sizewell

Framlingham

Leiston

Aldringham

Thorpeness

Kettleburgh

Hazlewood

Snape

Blaxhall

Aldeburgh

Stowmarket

Campsea Ash

Iken

Slaughden

Helmingham

Ufford

Rendlesham

Sudbourne

Bromeswell

Eyke

Wantisden

Chillesford

Melton

Tunstall

Butley

Orford

Woodbridge

Sutton Hoo

Gedgrave

Martlesham

Sutton

Tangham

Havergate Island

Sproughton

Capel St Andrew

Bramford

Shottisham

Boyton

Ipswich

Waldringfield

Hollesley

Wherestead

Hemley

Ramsholt

Alderton

Newbourne

Kirton

Woolverstone

Falkenham

Bawdsey

Levington

Walton

Felixstowe Ferry

Pin Mill

Trimley

Holbrook

Shotley

Felixstowe

Rough Towers

Landguard

Harwich

INTRODUCTION

This book is an attempt to paint a picture of the towns, villages, countryside and rivers of the Suffolk coast. It can be tempting to portray the Suffolk coastal area, in paint, photographs and words, as being simply beautiful views and wonderful countryside suitable for birds. In fact, it is a place where people live and which they feel strongly about and is an area that has often been in the front line of events.

The sea has pounded the Suffolk coast into its present shape while people have altered the countryside to fulfil their needs and ambitions. This coast does not exist in isolation, it is in close proximity to the rest of Western Europe, just across the North Sea, and to London, just to the south and these have been the major sources of influence. For a brief period in the early Anglo-Saxon period East Anglia was a self governing kingdom, but this did not last long. Although the county has long been part of the kingdom of England, and of Great Britain, it does have its own strong local identity. An identity created by a blend of outside influences, from the Anglo-Saxons to the bird empires, tempered by a local way of seeing things.

The term Sandlings, that covers the villages on the lightland between the Suffolk rivers, first appeared in print in the eighteenth century. I didn't hear the area being described as the Sandlings when I grew up here, but in 1986, when searching for a book title, I re-used the term in *The Suffolk Sandlings*. There is no clear boundary where the Sandlings Coast starts and finishes. Very generally it is the light land countryside between the estuaries and it extends as far inland as the A12 road. Before cars came into general use, the country villages between the rivers were remote and each peninsula had the atmosphere of an island. In 2002 when I wrote a book about the entire Suffolk coast up to Lowestoft, I searched again for a descriptive term for the whole coast and came up with *The Sunrise Coast*. It is after all the first part of the British Isles to see the sun rise every morning.

In compiling this book I have found some books useful, because they are based on original material, these include John Hewitt's *Two Horse Power*, Richard Pinney's *Smoked Salmon and Oysters* and Leonard P. Thompson's *Smugglers of the Suffolk Coast*. Jane Hart told me about her relations at Kessingland while John Chaplin reminded me about his smuggler ancestor on the River Ore and information on this river also came from George Watson of Chillesford and Stuart Bacon at Orford. Marcus Gladwell talked about the River Blyth. Arthur Percival alerted me to the Dutch gables and I was surprised, once I got my eye in, to find so many in East Anglia. Further information came from Katie Howson of the East Anglian Traditional Music Trust and Pat Mitchell and Simon Leatherdale of the Forestry Commission. Frank Brown of Bawdsey talked to me about how he had introduced a computer to Ipswich. Tony Osler on Harold Smy. George Prior of Lowestoft reminisced about the Ipswich shipyard. Thanks to Ron Geater for showing us around his nurseries and John and Ann Bater for introducing us to him.

It is fascinating to research the past and equally enjoyable meeting people and working with those whose efforts help to create the finished book. My wife Pearl did not read the text until it was finished, but then helped to shape the work. However we both went on trips to research and take photographs. My son Jonathan had the presence of mind to grab the camera in somewhat bumpy conditions to take the photograph of the *Three Sisters* coming over the Deben Bar and I took the rest of the photographs. For the editing I must once again thank Diana McMillan. Thanks too to the staff of the printers, The Lavenham Press, who are expert at giving a book a polished finish.

RS
Ramsholt 2009.

Early one August morning in 2008 the *Sea Stallion*, a 30m long replica of a Viking longship, left the Heritage Quay at Lowestoft and headed home across the North Sea for Roskilde in Denmark. Most of her crew of sixty were at the oars, but as she left the harbour the crew all stood up and let out a Viking roar. The Danish crew came in friendship in their longship from Roskilde Museum, but their Viking ancestors came to rob the Anglo-Saxons and were quite happy to murder them in the process. East Anglians are very proud of their Viking ancestry, but the sight of a longship with a crew letting out their battle roar, a thousand years ago, would have been very bad news.

The longships were the Danish Vikings' secret weapons. With them they came across the North Sea unannounced and arrived in force to loot and pillage towns and villages at will. The Anglo-Saxons could not organize themselves to repel these sudden attacks; at least not until Alfred the Great and his sons turned Wessex into a military state.

The *Sea Stallion* is a replica of a troop carrier that voyaged and waged war all over Europe. Ironically these super longships were an invention of Alfred the Great. Alfred realised that the way to overcome the raiding Vikings was to beat them at their own game and build larger longships. The vanquished Vikings went home and, in time, increased the size of their fighting longships from about 21m to about 30m.

The *Sea Stallion*, (*Havhingsten fra Glendalough*, in Danish) averaged about 6-7 knots under sail on her long voyage from Roskilde to Dublin, but made 14 knots with perfect conditions. Under oar the crew of sixty rowed every third oar for half an hour and then had an hour's rest. The longest she was rowed at a stretch on the Dublin to Lowestoft trip was six hours. However, there

Looking down the River Alde, towards Iken Church. The Norman Church at Iken is probably where St Botolph established his Icanhoe Monastery in 654, but the wooden buildings appear to have been destroyed in the winter of 869-70 when a Viking fleet moved along the East Coast looting churches.

was always endless bailing to get rid of water that came over the rail.

The *Sea Stallion* was not the first Viking replica to suddenly appear on the Suffolk Coast. In 1997 I had a telephone message to say that a Finnish Viking replica had appeared in Lowestoft harbour and that her crew had had a tough crossing and was asked to see if I could help them. We arrived at the Trawl Dock to find Rus Project's 37ft *Heimlosa Rus*, a replica of the Lapuri longship that had been found on the sea bed. The crew of a trawler had taken pity on them, in the way that seamen all over the world do, and given them hot food and showers.

The Rus Project came from the Swedish speaking part of Finland and wanted to prove their Viking ancestry. The previous summer the Rus Project had left Finland, but their first longship was wrecked in Denmark so they went home and built another one and set off again. She was very authentic with horse hair rigging and the crew sleeping under animals' skins. The only modern feature was a chest aft full of charts, compass and radio.

After leaving southern Denmark it had taken them four days to cover the 320 miles to Lowestoft. At one point it had blown Force 6 and they were all soaked in the driving rain and had to bail continually. The Vikings actually considered a ship safe to go to sea in if it could be kept afloat by two people bailing out. One problem the Vikings didn't have to cope with was the gas rigs; the *Heimlosa Rus* crew had had to row very hard to avoid being swept into gas platforms. When they reached the Suffolk coast these Baltic sailors were amazed at the force of the tide.

There were seven people on *Heimlosa Rus*, six Finns and one Swede. It was the Swedish mate who spoke English and was glad to see us. 'Take me to a farmer's field' he demanded, but I sought more clarification of his need. It turned

The River Blyth with black-headed gulls nesting. In the distance is the Holy Trinity parish church at Blythburgh. To the right of the church tower, in the trees beside the river, is the site of the Anglo-Saxon Minster of Blythburgh. This wooden building does not appear to have been destroyed by the Vikings and was later replaced by the Normans with stone buildings, but it was not a rich monastery. Blythburgh was an important place when there was a Kingdom of East Anglia, but with the loss of Dunwich the area became impoverished.

In 2005 a boat was burnt on Aldeburgh beach as an event for school children. November 5 has always been a bad day for historic boats and in the 1980s a group in the 'Bell' at Walberswick hit on the idea of burning a boat near the parish dock as a fund raising event. There was not however a tradition of boat burning on the Suffolk coast.

The *Sea Stallion*, the 70m replica of a Viking longship, at the Heritage Quay, Lowestoft, 2008.

The Vikings of Middle England, a re-enactment group, giving a display of hand-to-hand fighting at Woodbridge.

out that they had really suffered from the lack of hot food and wanted to make a fire box.

I took him to Covehithe brickworks, a wonderful collection of traditional buildings, which produce Suffolk red bricks. Here they happily gave him a sack of clay. Back at Lowestoft a box was made and the clay put in it on which they made an open fire for cooking. A difficult way to cook in an open wooden boat at sea, but at least they got a hot drink in calm weather. Going to sea in an open boat is a great deal tougher than putting to sea with decked craft.

The *Heimlosa Rus* sailed on and got into a little trouble with the tide in the Straits of Dover and was towed out of the way of ferries, but she reached Devon. Later they crossed to the River Seine, through France round to the Bosporus, across the Black Sea, up the rivers of Russia and arrived home after three summers. A longship was not a comfortable way to make sea voyages, but, with skill and luck, they proved it was achievable.

On the passage to Dublin the *Sea Stallion* had problems with her side rudder and this was solved by fitting a block and tackle to control

what is basically a great side steering paddle. It may be that the ships from the early medieval period had the same problem because two steering rudders have turned up on the Suffolk coast. A Southwold fisherman trawled one up, dating from around 820. Since it was a decent piece of oak it was kept and it was not until it reached the Ferry Quay at Woodbridge to be cut up that someone realized what it really was. In 1987 Nobby Hutton found another side rudder on the beach at Easton Broad, after a gale. These rudders were mounted on the starboard side, literally the 'steer board' side, no doubt because most men steered with their right hand.

These early side rudders might have come from local Anglo-Saxon ships engaged in normal trade or fishing. Another early clinker boat turned up at Sizewell in 2008. A dig was undertaken by the Suffolk County Council Archaeological Service on the site of a new plant to handle the electricity coming ashore from the Great Gabbard Wind Farm, the world's largest wind farm on sandbanks off the Suffolk coast.

Sizewell is another name to add to the list of Suffolk places that have gone into the sea. Sizewell was always part of Leiston, but had its own market, started in 1237, some seventy-five years before Leiston had a market. In the 1300s

The road to nowhere. This road leaves Covehithe and used to go to the village of Southmere, out on Covehithe Ness. The Ness, like Covehithe Haven, has long since gone into the sea.

Looking south from Covehithe to Southwold, 2007. When the Vikings came this was all land and Covehithe Haven ran inland. When St Andrew's Church, Covehithe was built it was about three miles from the coast, it is now barely half a mile. The wealth to build such a church probably came through herring fishing from Covehithe Haven, now completely eroded away. The Suffolk coast had been a wealthy, populated area, but when huge sections of land slipped into the sea, people moved away.

St John the Baptist Church at Butley stands almost alone in what were formerly open sheep walks. The early Christian Church divided the countryside up into parishes and most of the villages in the Sandlings have Anglo-Saxon names, which suggests that many local people survived the Viking invasion.

Leiston Abbey moved some of its Sizewell tenants inland to new areas because of sea erosion and flooding forced Leiston Abbey to be re-sited further inland. Over the next three hundred years Sizewell went slowly into the sea, so that by the 1600 very little was left. The area excavated would have been an industrial area, just inland from the town under the sea. The remains of the clinker boat found had been used to line a well.

The Sizewell boat, excavated by Robert Atfield, dates from around 1300 and Richard Darrah believed it must have been around 23ft long and was built of oak clinker planks a foot wide. These planks had been skilfully split from a tree trunk and fastened with iron rivets, with hair 'luting', to prevent leaking, between the planks. Before being broken up the boat had been much repaired and had probably been used for longshore fishing off Sizewell. It must have been built seven hundred years after the famous Sutton Hoo longship, but building methods were more or less the same.

When the Vikings arrived on this coast Sizewell may have been one of several small havens that have since been eaten away by the sea. The Vikings probably gave the name to Thorpe, which was altered to Thorpeness when it became the mock Tudor seaside holiday village in the early twentieth century. When the Vikings came here the Hundred River emptied into Thorpe Haven. The Haven was a wide, shallow estuary, but in the Elizabethan era the silt being dragged down the coast closed off the mouth so that ships couldn't use it. The Haven turned into grazing marshes.

Thorpe appears to be a Viking name and the haven here would have been just the sort of place they liked to use as a base for raiding. The Vikings would have worried that the local people would make a surprise attack and Thorpe Haven was ideal because they could enter and leave quickly if an attack was mounted on them. To begin with the Danish Vikings had been making summer raiding voyages, but in 865 they adopted a new plan. A large fleet of longships arrived in East Anglia with the intention of over wintering and capturing as much of the British Isles as they could get, as their own territory.

Part of the reason Vikings attacked the British Isles was because on the European mainland Christian armies had begun to push up into the pagan north. The Vikings saw the people in the British Isles as betrayers of the old faith. The monasteries, which were known to contain gold and precious objects, were prime targets for Vikings. They burnt and sacked monasteries along the Suffolk coast. Since the monks were great keepers of records those fires probably consumed most of the accounts of the Anglo-Saxon Kingdom of East Anglia.

The Viking army captured the whole of East Anglia to use it as a base for attacking other English kingdoms. Part of this was the murder of Edmund, King of the East Angles, in 869. Edmund knew the game was up and his forces were overrun by the Viking Ivar and his army encamped at Thetford. Edmund's armour-bearer was an eye-witness to his end. Ivar's army was ravaging through Norfolk and sent a message to Edmund that they wanted him to hand over the kingship. Edmund replied that he would if they converted to Christianity. The Vikings promptly turned up and tied Edmund to a tree and tortured him to death. Since he refused, under pain of death, to give up his faith, Edmund was made a major saint by the medieval church.

The Danish Vikings whole philosophy of life was devoted to battle and conquest, but Suffolk had a good effect on them as they settled down and turned into farmers and fishermen. Most village names on the Suffolk coast are Anglo-Saxon, but names such as Ashby, Barnby, Lound, Risby and Somerleyton are probably places where the Norse men settled.

Eyke is another village name that is thought to date back to the Norse settlers. Originally Rendlesham had extended down to Sutton, the 'New Estate.' The parishes of Eyke and Bromeswell were carved out of part of the old royal parish of Rendlesham. When the Anglo-Saxons came to Suffolk in the late 500s their probable first conquest was the country around Rendlesham. This Celtic sub-kingdom was later known as the Wicklaw (Uicchelaue). When the Norse army took over the whole of East Anglia a Danish earl administered this province from Sudbourne, until the Anglo-Saxons pushed the Norse out of eastern England.

The Vikings contributed little to the growth of East Anglia, in fact they had destroyed a great deal, but their fighting spirit and secret weapons, the longships, remained large in the public's imagination. A few years ago some people sailing off Kessingland suddenly saw a Viking longship through the mist and then it was gone. Then there are people at Brightlingsea who believe they saw a Viking ghost ship going silently up the creek one night. The Vikings are long gone, but never forgotten.

Looking across the dewpond at Church Farm, Kettleburgh towards St Andrews Church. Some moats and ponds were dug for building material, but many medieval manor houses were surrounded by a moat. The moat was there, particularly in famine years, to safeguard the manor's grain and livestock against theft. Because the countryside is so open there was a constant threat from thieves and modern farms still have this problem.

All Saints Church at Ramsholt used to stand in the middle of a late Anglo-Saxon village by a creek. The Normans built the round tower after the Viking raids finished.

The 'White Hart Inn' at Blythburgh has Dutch gables on one end. In about 1976 the 'White Hart' was one of the first village pubs in East Suffolk to start serving good meals. When Blythburgh's only shop closed in 2001 the landlord of the 'White Hart Inn,' Michael Davis, converted the coal barn beside the pub into a post office and shop.

The cooling water that is pumped back into the sea from the power station reactors is reputed to make the sea several degrees warmer. This attracts anglers to fish off Sizewell beach.

I huddled over the tiller of *Sea Fever* without too much certainty of exactly where I was going. It was about 1.30 in the morning and dark and although it was July it was very cold. The fresh breeze was pushing our little gaff cutter along at speed. I was nineteen years old and had just sailed my little clinker cutter across the North Sea. To be honest I wouldn't go far from the Deben in *Sea Fever* now but then I was young and thirsting for adventure under sail. I loved this little converted ship's lifeboat, but her engine had given up early on the passage and resulted in a slow North Sea crossing. Now, making my first foreign port under my own command, I was approaching a blaze of lights on the north shore of the River Schelde that my chart said was Flushing.

Under my bidding, and in a fresh breeze, *Sea Fever* ploughed through the water of the River Wester Schelde towards the low lights of Flushing. I thought that, as we were under sail only, I could go into the largest dock, so that I had room to tack about. Then I heard the heavy thump of a big diesel engine and out

of the darkness appeared a big Dutch tug. On the bow was a Dutchman shouting 'Englander, Englander!' We were heading for the big commercial harbour and our new friend on the Dutch tug was telling us to go to a small harbour further up river.

Next morning, after some sleep, tied up to a jetty, we began asking for an engineer to get the engine functioning again. In the afternoon a cheerful Dutchman turned up with a bag of tools and began to strip down the engine. He got it going, although that little petrol Stuart Turner was never much good. When I asked the cheerful Dutchman how much I owed him he was quite offended at the idea. He had not mended it for money, but because we were English in trouble. He had fought in the Royal Navy in World War II and this was his way of repaying our nation.

When he left, he squeezed my hand and said 'Next time you are in Liverpool say hello to my mate Nobby for me.' I asked weakly where Nobby lived, but he laughed and said 'everyone knows Nobby!'

I never did meet Nobby and was embarrassed by the engineer's act of generosity; the three of us were far too young to have played any part in the liberation of The Netherlands from Nazi Occupation. For the rest of that cruise we were frequently the objects of generosity from the Dutch. I have over the decades tried to repay them, but I never could repay those wonderful kind people we met in 1957.

The purpose of this piece of personal nostalgia is to show that it does not take long to cross the North Sea from Suffolk, even in a small un-sophisticated sailing craft. In the Anglo-Saxon period there was regular trade from Ipswich across the North Sea and up the Rhine. In the medieval period the Wool Trade was England's main industry and ships took wool to the vast market at Bruges, but not straight across the North Sea. The Wool Trade was strictly controlled by a series of monopolies by the Guilds and the King. Wool had to be shipped to London and then to Calais and then into the Low Countries to be woven and then taken on to European markets.

When the Catholic rulers of France and the Low Countries engaged in some 'ethnic cleansing' of their Protestant subjects many moved north to the Netherlands, or took a short passage across the North Sea and settled in south-eastern England. These Flemish emigrants brought with them cloth weaving skills which in time increased the earning power of the Wool Towns of East Anglia.

It is believed that ships returning from the European markets brought bricks and tiles with them, as well as bags of gold for the merchants. In East Anglia, which had very little natural stone and was rapidly using up its supply of oak, bricks were soon adopted. With the bricks of the Low Countries came a new style of architecture. Kent has many houses with 'Dutch gables,' but East Anglia has more.

The Dutch-style gables appear in two distinct styles. First, curly gables appeared in big country houses in the late Elizabethan and Jacobean periods. These were architect designed, although we don't know the names of the architects. The Dutch gable then 'went native' and started to be used on ordinary farmhouses, town houses and even mills. Victorian builders reintroduced the Dutch gable because they loved any elaborate embellishment and it seemed to be a native style from the past. In the 1930s and even in many modern houses Dutch gables give a feeling of style from the past.

By the eighteenth century the great landowners, who had been on the Grand Tour to Italy, introduced the 'classic' styles of the Roman Empire for their country houses. By the late eighteenth century the Suffolk coastal area had its own style of red brick cottages and farmhouses. These have curved 'eye lid' window tops and often a brick ridge on the eves of the rooves. Could this ridge have been the last vestige of a Dutch gable?

There had been smuggling in the days of the restricted practices of the Wool Trade, but when the Government slapped heavy duties on luxury goods, smuggling of spirits, tobacco and silks became big business. Flushing, at the mouth of the Wester Schelde, became the centre of smuggling to the East Coast. Here goods could be bought and smugglers hid out when the English coast became 'too hot' for them. It was here that the captains of the smuggling luggers bought their geneva gin and tobacco.

The great era of smuggling was between about 1770-1820 and no other activity has made such a strong impact on the coastal villages. It is over two hundred years since the smuggling gangs

were stamped out, but some tales have lived on. Although smuggling was a brutal criminal activity, making high profits for those involved, the majority of people on the East Coast were either in league with the smugglers or at least had sympathy with them. The farmers turned a blind eye to the fact that their horses were taken from the stables at night and used to transport 'goods' inland.

One account is that the farmer Cross at Hemley Hall used to come in to breakfast swearing because the smugglers had used his horses in the night and they were unfit for a day's farm work. This ties up with the local legend that smugglers hid goods in caves in the Ramsholt Cliff, just across the Rocks Reach on the Deben from Hemley Hall, and then transported it at night into Ipswich. These caves have long since eroded away, but another legend is that Ramsholt Church was used by smugglers to store goods, certainly in the eighteenth century this lonely parish had been visited by few people.

The usual stories of smugglers are that they landed 'goods', Dutch gin, tobacco and silk on the open coast. As this required good weather they often landed their 'goods' in the estuaries. The legend in the Paice family is that one of their forebears farmed at Falkenham and once, while walking across the marshes on a Sunday afternoon with his family, Mr Paice suddenly bent down and pulled out a little barrel of spirits from under a bridge. His reward for letting the smugglers use his land and horses.

Gwen Dyke, a teacher with a passion for recording Suffolk's past, met an old lady who had a little barrel that had been given to her great-grandmother. She had been the daughter of the landlord of the Butley 'Oyster,' and had been given this barrel by the smugglers for keeping quiet. Another old lady had told her how she had 'danced for the smugglers' in a barn at Kenton.

The Sizewell boat *Joseph William*. Many days are lost, due to bad weather, when boats are used for fishing off the beach.

The Coast Guard station, at Sizewell Gap. The Gap was originally between cliffs that have long since eroded away.

The smugglers relied on good information about the movements of the Revenue Men. The Dunwich smuggler Isaac Larter used to hang a lantern in the ruins on the cliff when 'the coast was clear.' Dumboy Cottage, on the sharp bend on the road from Hollesley out across the marshes to Shingle Street, is said to have been the home of a dumb man who was trusted by the smugglers because they knew he could never tell the Revenue their secret movements. Gwen Dyke's comment was that a deaf man had lived here much later, so this may have just been a legend.

By going into the rivers the smugglers were more liable to be caught. In 1738 a smugglers' sloop ran aground on the Deben bar and the Revenue men walked out at low tide and captured them. On the Butley River the Collins's of Button's Farm, Capel St Andrew, used to put a light out to tell the son of the house, who was master of a smuggling craft, that the coast was clear of Revenue men. Once they shone a light, without knowing that the Revenue men were lying in wait in the Butley River. Too late the cutter sailed into the narrow river, only to realise it was a trap. Fighting broke out and one Revenue man was shot dead, but the smugglers knew they were about to be overpowered. Most of smugglers got ashore and ran away, but Collins, the master of the cutter, tried to get his craft back into the River Ore and escape. In fact the cutter went ashore and he was captured and later hanged for a murder he had not actually committed. This account no doubt lived on because the family felt a great sense of injustice.

Hangings took place on the hill beside Wilford Hollows, over looking Wilford Bridge. The site of the gallows was destroyed just after World War II by a quarry. When the authorities were worried that smugglers would mount an armed rescue, the prisoners were hanged in Melton Jail, which, if I remember rightly, was an Elizabethan building in Melton Street that

was demolished in the 1960s and replaced by houses.

There clearly were 'runs' on the open coast because the legend lived on that smugglers had come up Beach Lane, Alderton with goods landed on the shingle beach of Hollesley Bay. It appears that the goods had been hidden in the parish church because there is a brick tunnel leading to the nearby farmhouse of Alderton Hall. Once the Revenue men seized two carts of brandy at Melton, but the Alderton and Bawdsey gang, some forty men, got away. Another time the Revenue seized goods belonging to the Orford smuggler John Cook, but he led his gang in an attack on the barn where they were stored and got them back. Rough old days.

The scale of the smuggling operation is breathtaking. Sizewell Gap saw some of the largest 'crops' landed. In 1745 the Hadleigh gang were regularly landing here. In May, well-armed men protected and helped with the landing of dry goods from Cobbe's cutter, ferried ashore by local boats, the whole operation took about seven hours. A week later Cobbe was back again and sixty horses carried the goods inland. At Benacre Warren the Norwich and Yarmouth gangs joined forces with a hundred men and 120 horses to land goods. In all the Revenue men calculated that 4,551 horse loads of contraband were landed on Suffolk beaches that year. It was hardly an undercover operation, but the Revenue Service didn't have enough men to overpower the gangs. Even if the smugglers were caught, they could pay a fine and buy their way out of jail.

It was not always easy sailing for the smuggling gangs. In 1775 the Dragoons seized fifteen carts and forty horses, carrying some 2,400 gallons and bags of tea, at Sizewell Gap. By this time smuggling had become a local industry, one that was sustained with violence. Even now it is not difficult to imagine the smugglers' lugger hovering into view on the horizon and the men and horses standing on the beach.

The tide against the smuggling gangs turned when the wars with Napoleon's France ended and the Government had the resources and time to organize coastal watches. There are many court records about the convictions of men caught smuggling, but virtually nothing is known about the men who organized and led these gangs.

One glimpse, through the mists of time, of the 'free traders' came in 1785 when Richard Chaplin (1751-1833) of Orford advertised that he was giving up smuggling and was selling off all the equipment needed for running contraband. To have openly publicised smuggling, a criminal activity, showed the double standards of the eighteenth century when money and rank could by-pass the law. Richard Chaplin appears to have used the profits from smuggling to buy Cowton Farm, Sudbourne and his family were there until William Chaplin sold up in about 1900. Cowton Farm had its own dock on the River Alde, but this appears to have been cut much later for the Victorian sailing barges taking mangolds, straw and hay to London and returning with horse muck for the fields.

There are many glimpses of the romantic age of smuggling, but few complete stories. It appears every coastal village had a gang, organized in the pubs, but mysterious backers had purchased the 'goods' in Holland and eventually sold it. The gap in our knowledge of smugglers was filled in by fiction. In 1845 Rev Richard Cobbold, the Rector of Wortham, published his novel 'The History of Margaret Catchpole, a Suffolk Girl' about the adventures of a country girl who fell in love with the leader of a Suffolk smuggling gang. Cobbold claimed 'the public may depend upon the truth of the main feature of this narrative.' He clearly never thought his romantic novel would ever be subjected to informed research, but even in Cobbold's lifetime people were saying that most of it was fiction.

There really was a serving girl called Margaret Catchpole, who had worked for Cobbold's mother and then in the Ipswich waterfront. It was absolutely true that Margaret dressed up as a man and stole one of Cobbold's horses and rode to London, but was caught when she was trying to sell the horse. For this she was sentenced to death, but she escaped from Ipswich jail, was recaptured and transported to Australia. Cobbold's imagination kicked in when he tried to work out why she had embarked on a ride to London. In his mind the cause of the trouble had to be a man, so he came up with the explanation that she had stolen a horse so that she could meet her lover Will Laud, leader of a smuggling gang.

There is no evidence that Will Laud or his gang ever existed. Also the real Margaret Catchpole was older and tougher than the innocent country girl in Cobbold's yarn. Cobbold might well have been telling a kind of truth, basing his novel on the stories about smugglers he had heard as young man in Ipswich. In the novel the smuggler's hideout is in a cave in the cliff at Bawdsey. In the 1950s the story in Bawdsey was that this cave was reached by going down a well at what was then called Lower Barn, but became Dairy Farm where Lady Quilter kept her Red Poll cows to supply milk to Bawdsey Manor. The cliff has eroded back, but there is a dip that might have been where there was a cave.

The real-life Margaret Catchpole could have had little idea that she would be transformed by the book, which appeared long after her death, into the heroine of the Suffolk Coast. Although soon after she was jailed, a play appeared on the London stage about impersonating a man to steal a horse, which fascinated the public. After a time in Sydney she moved inland, slightly away from the sticky heat of the coast, to Richmond, NSW which was just opening up as a wheat-growing area. Here she appears to have been well-liked, and worked as a servant to a doctor and as a midwife. She never married, which was unusual for the time, and there is no record of her having any interest in men. In the twentieth century the gutsy girl in Cobbold's story fascinated the Australians and the first feature film made in this new nation was about Margaret Catchpole. Here she was seen as the poor convict who made good in a new land, although nobody could work out quite why she stole the horse. That and more remained Margaret's secret, but money is always useful.

The first cruising yachtsmen to cross the North Sea overlapped with the romantic age of smuggling. When the early British yachts, such as the 3ton *Helen* of Woodbridge which was sailed single handed to Holland by Thomas Grimwood in 1851, arrived in the Wester

Schlede there would still have been men alive who had helped load the smuggler's luggers.

In the first half of the nineteenth century Coast Guards were stationed all around the coast, often in guard ships, usually former Royal Navy vessels, permanently anchored in the estuaries. These were replaced with cottages for the Coast Guards that were built all around the coast and by then the public had lost their sympathy for the lawless smuggling gangs. The Coast Guard's brass telescopes were trained on the horizon and became an early warning system for both unwelcome vessels approaching the shore and vessels in trouble.

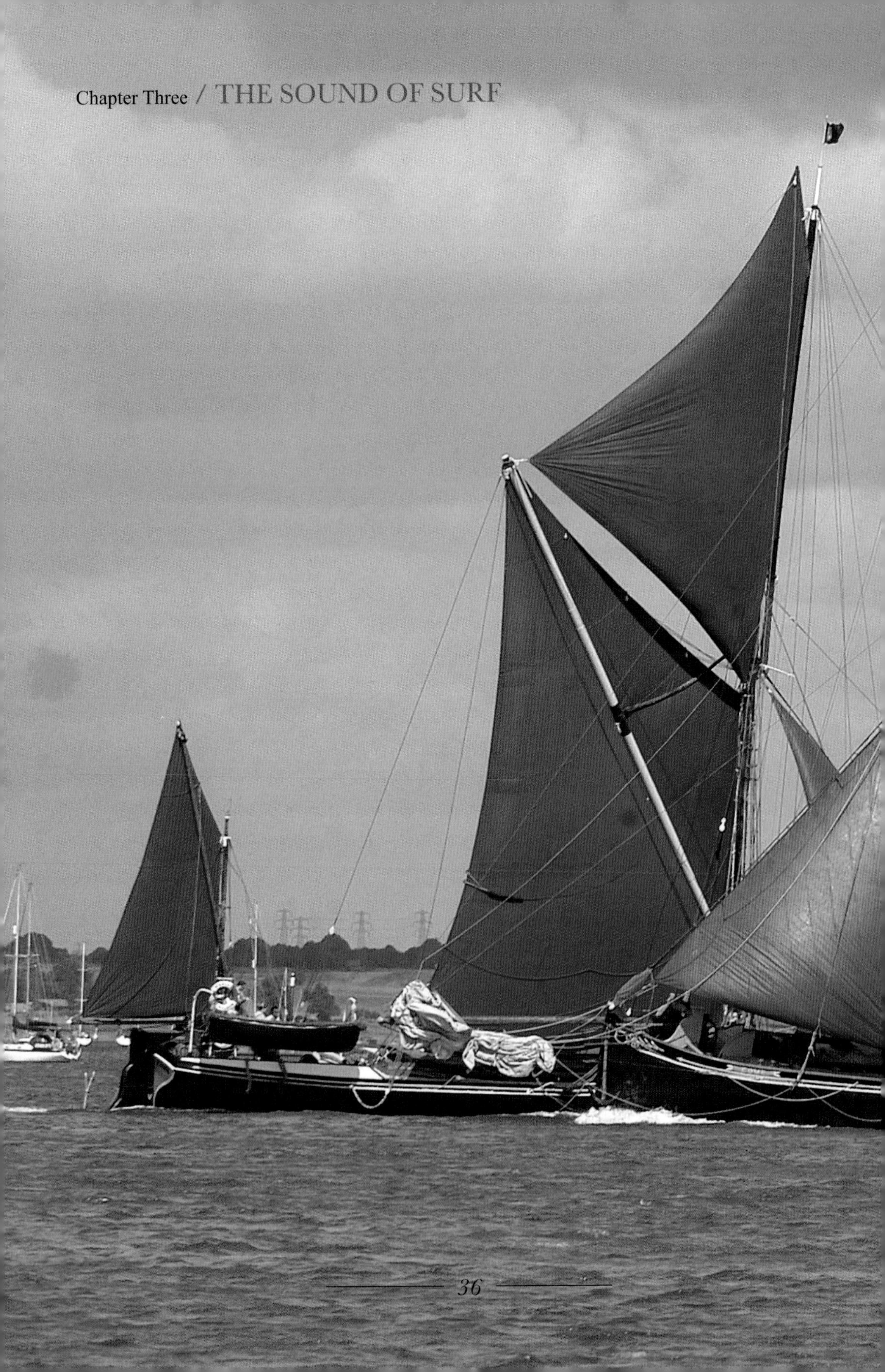

The spritsail barges *Mirosa* and *Edme* at the start of the 2008 Pin Mill Barge Match.

Sailing barges in Ipswich Dock during the week before the Pin Mill Barge Match, 2008. The last regular trade from Ipswich Dock ended in 2004. This was malt, from Paul's maltings to Becks Brewery, Germany.

One night in July, 1960 we berthed alongside the Harwich dredger *Landguard* in *Sea Fever*. The dredger's great grey hull shielded us from the rising wind and in the morning, when I intended to sail back to the Deben, it was blowing about force 6-7 south west, not a good idea to go to sea in a small boat, even for a short distance in that wind. Instead we went up the River Orwell to Woolverstone and as we picked up a mooring, a sailing barge came past. I think it was Cranfield's barge *Venture*, deeply loaded with wheat from the Royal Docks, London, bound for the mills at the head of Ipswich Dock. Her sails were worn and her hull paint dull, a sharp contrast to the smart yachts on their moorings off the Royal Harwich Yacht Club. Ipswich was the last port in northern Europe to have a fleet of commercial sailing vessels, a point that the port managers tried to play down at the time. They, quite rightly, wanted their port to be seen as progressive.

Between 1820 and 1908, some 160 sailing barges, mostly built of wood, were built at Ipswich and the last one was the 85ft *Ardwina*. Read & Page built two iron spritsail barges, 51ft *Ironsides* in 1841 and the slightly larger *Gipping* in 1842 to carry beer from Stowmarket to London. For the tow up the Ipswich & Stowmarket Navigation, horses were hired from a carter with stables in the 'Bull' inn, just behind Ipswich Custom House. After Navigation to Stowmarket closed, Packard's steam barges towed lighters up to their fertilizer plant at Bramford until 1922. Before the River Orwell was dredged above Woolverstone, ships went on the Butterman's Bay buoys, just below Pin Mill. Here, grain was discharged into sailing barges and Gipping barges to go up to the Ipswich mills. Packard's steam barge *Trent River*, built by Orvis & Co in 1916, was the last cargo carrier built at Ipswich.

R & W Paul kept their sailing barges *Marjorie* and *Anglia* until 1960 and Cranfield Bros barges

The 30-ton River Gipping barge *Yare*, was built by Orvis, at Ipswich, in 1891. When the Ipswich and Stowmarket Navigation closed in 1922 the *Yare* was used in the Orwell ballast trade for another ten years. Jack Haste has owned and used the *Yare* as a houseboat for many years.

May and *Venture* carried a few freights under sail until about 1963. Their barge *Spinaway C*, which was used for lightering and racing in the last few years, was sold in 1967. The very last trading sailing barge owned on the Orwell was the 91ft wooden *Cambria* owned and skippered by Bob Roberts, who lived at Pin Mill. She ploughed her lonely way under sail only until she delivered her final cargo to the ECF Mill in Ipswich in 1970.

In 1974 Pauls rigged out their barge *Ena* again to sail as a company social barge. When they sold her in 1998. Pauls had owned the barge for ninety-two years, since they had bought her new from the builders at Harwich. Pauls also owned the Dock End Shipyard where their wooden barges went for repair. When the barge fleets had finally gone the yard was modernised by Liverpool Seaforth Group. In 1990 George Prior, who had trained at Brooke Marine and operated ship repair yards at Lowestoft, Swansea and Hull, took over the Ipswich yard. At Ipswich

steel vessels of up to 800 tons and 80m long, providing they drew nothing forward, could be hauled up the slipway. Just as the barges had been driven out of trade because they were too small; George Prior found that larger vessels were taking on the short sea trades and making the coastal vessels he was repairing redundant. He closed the Dock End Yard, Ipswich in 2003.

The best time to see barges on the River Orwell is about the time of the Pin Mill Barge Match, a race that has taken place annually since 1962. These barges are mostly 'charter' vessels, working as passenger carriers. Because barges are very beautiful under sail, the public have remained aware of them, but Suffolk's other traditional wooden working craft, the longshore fishing boats working off beaches, appear to be passing away unnoticed. Russell and Brian Upson were regularly building wooden boats at Slaughden Quay, Aldeburgh and Brian developed a fibre-glass version of the Suffolk

The Thorpeness boat *Pet* drift netting for herring. The herring arrive on the East Anglian coast in the autumn and stay until the following spring.

Robert Simper on his Suffolk beach boat *Three Sisters* crossing the Deben Bar, 2008. This boat was built in 1896 and was fished off Thorpeness beach until about 1952. She was rebuilt in 1994 after laying derelict in Ralph Brinkley's yard at Orford.

Steve King's *Jill Ann* landing on Dunwich beach, 2008. This was the only full time boat fishing off the beach then, but another grp boat was worked part time. That year forty-five boats were fishing from the Suffolk coast, mostly from Lowestoft, and there were about twenty part timers.

The beach fishing boat *Shady Nook* all alone on Thorpeness beach with Aldeburgh in the background, 2008. The *Shady Nook* had been built by Everson of Woodbridge in 1955 and was kept out in the open on Thorpeness beach for over fifty years.

John Westrup, Tony Ralph and Graham Westrup with their 16ft beach boat *Shady Nook*, the last fishing boat on Thorpeness beach, 2008.

In about 1910 there were fourteen men working boats off Thorpeness beach and in the 1950s Tim Brown and Percy Westrup were the last full time fishermen. In 1968 John Westrup and Tony Ralph bought the *Shady Nook* and worked from the beach, mainly potting for crab and lobster. John's son Graham fished her until 2005 and then used the grp *Gill-Jan*, but when the beach became steeper the boat was moved to Southwold harbour.

The former Kessingland boat *Valsand* in Southwold Harbour.

beach boat, but Frank Knights of Woodbridge built the last wooden beach boat, *Dodger* for 'Dodger' Holmes, at Dunwich, in 1993.

In 1964 I was talking to a retired fishermen in the Reading Room at Southwold and he told me that before World War II there had been a hundred boats fishing off Southwold beach. Suffolk longshore fishermen often found other jobs as well, but they all returned for the autumn sprat fishery, which was their 'harvest.' The Suffolk beach fishermen caught herring for the local market, but couldn't compete with the huge catches landed at Lowestoft so they concentrated on sprat. The Southwold boats were open clinker 'punts' which two men crewed for trawling and three men for drift netting. This meant that in the sprat season some three hundred men and boys were earning a hard living from the beaches at Southwold.

Once when the Southwold boats were at sea, my fishermen friend told me, when they were caught by a sudden gale from the north,

a direction they all feared because in the steep seas, they could not return to land on the beach. Instead the heavily reefed little luggers had to run south around Orfordness. Here they went up the River Ore to Orford. The men telegraphed home that they were all safe and pulled their boats up on the beach and lived under the sails for ten days until the weather was fine enough for them to return to Southwold.

Billy English, who lived in a cottage beside the 'Bell' at Walberswick, told me that when he started fishing in 1927 he once counted eighty-seven punts trawling off Southwold. He wanted to buy his own boat so he joined a Lowestoft steam drifter for sixteen weeks and when he came home he bought the 18ft *Maud Ellen* for £8, complete with trawl and a shrimp trawl.

Southwold had a sloping beach but erosion made it steeper and too difficult to land the boats. Once the 'punts' were fitted with engines the fishermen began to use the Harbour as a base. To start with they used to haul the boats

The 'punt' *Dodger* in Southwold Harbour. At Southwold the open clinker longshore fishing boats are called 'punts.' because they are almost flat-bottomed. After the punts, fishermen adopted decked wooden boats, and in 1991 the fishermen changed over to smaller grp boats, to be within the quota regulations. By 2009 fast grp catamarans were being tried.

out with hand capstans, as they had done on the beach, but by 1932 more jetties were being built. During World War II the harbour was closed because of the threat of a German invasion, and about twenty boats returned to fish off the beach. However after the War they moved back to the harbour, but by the 1970s some of the older boats were still laying between the beach huts on Southwold sea front.

I have tried to find a single Suffolk beach boat that has acquired any degree of fame or recognition. The nearest I have come up with is the Kessingland boat *Valsand* LT 311 which was chartered by the BBC producer Philip Donnellan, in 1955, to make a radio programme in the series 'Down to the Sea.' As the beach boats just worked in the waters close to their beach landing, *Valsand's* skipper, 'Hurricane' Brown, had not initially been keen on a trip along the coast, but he and his 72 year old mate Alf Brown eventually agreed.

The *Valsand*, very much smartened up

for her appearance on the BBC sound radio, left Southwold for her voyage up to Norfolk. The *Valsand* had been built as a motor boat at Lowestoft in 1948, but a lug foresail and mizzen was found so that at least half the trip could be made under sail. The use of sails added a bit of nostalgia to the trip, and with the engine off they could record their commentary as they went along the coast to Burnham Overy Staithe, over the next five days. Although this little trip is long forgotten, at the time, when BBC radio was the only public broadcasting medium, it was listened to by most of the inhabitants of the British Isles. After her brief moment of glory the *Valsand* returned to be used for sprat, herring and mackerel drifting, and shrimp trawling from 'Kess'el' beach. She has been kept in Southwold harbour for many decades since.

Kessingland produced another piece of modest fame with Stanley 'Cock Robin' Brown. In the 1930s workmen started digging a well at the foot of the cliff near Rider Haggard Lane

The old and new longshore fishing boats on Aldeburgh beach, 2009. Colin 'Toosie' Smith's wooden beach boat *Rachael Linda* and Richard Goldsmith's fibre-glass catamaran *Rockley*.

but it collapsed and trapped the workmen. 'Cock Robin' Brown, a young fisherman, was lowered down and dug them out. This might have passed unnoticed, except for the keen eye of Edward James Hunt who kept the shop at Kessingland's beach village. He was a 'stringer', supplying news stories for the nation press in London for 7/6 (seven shillings and six pence). Hunt was quickly on the beach snapping photographs of 'Cock Robin' for the benefit of the national press.

When 'Cock Robin' started fishing off Kessingland in the 1920s there were twenty-eight boats, between about 16-20ft long, working off the beach, and like the other Suffolk beach landings between Pakefield and Shingle Street, drifting was their main fishery. If they found a shoal they would, in fine weather, load boats down so that only the top plank was above water and then row back. Once when no shoals were coming into the inshore fishery the Kessingland boat *Bessie* was sailed out into the North Sea

where they met a returning steam drifter crewed by Kessingland men. They filled the *Bessie* up with herring and she sailed back into Lowestoft fish market and sold the catch. They then loaded the boat up with a ton of coal, sailed back to Kessingland and sold that.

In the 1960s 'Cock Robin's' boat *Result*, the last longshore boat built in Kessingland, sat perched on the edge of the beach in front of the fisherman's club. Inside the club at Kessingland the walls were covered in paintings by 'pier head artists' of sailing ships from that glorious era of sailing work-boats just before World War I. This club was left over from the fishermen's beach companies that kept 'yawls', fast sailing private lifeboats, on the beach. In the nineteenth century they went off salvaging vessels in distress. In the age of sailing ships when huge fleets of colliers passed up and down the North Sea, salvage was big business. When I started off helping the Ramsholt boatman Arthur Hunt in the

early 1950s, he absolutely hated the long shore men. 'Salvage sharks' he called them, because the memory of the beach companies' salvaging activities lived on.

The last place where salvaging was regularly practiced was at Felixstowe Ferry, where fishermen towed yachts off that were stuck on the Deben Bar. Charlie Brinkley, who was the most successful of the Deben Salvagers, had a hut down on the yacht club point and sat there watching with a telescope. In the summer of 2002, when the Deben Bar entrance channel was very shallow, Duncan Read said that he was towing about two yachts off every day at high tide. The advent of echo sounders and reliable charts has not quite ended the 'nice little towing jobs', because at Easter 2009 John White said that four yachts ran aground on the Bar.

While the story of fishing and boat building on the Suffolk coast has been about decline, Felixstowe Ferry seems to have slightly bucked the trend. Andy Moore has been fitting out a series of new hulls for commercial fishing, and in 2008 he built the new steel 43ton mooring barge cat *Deben Trojan* which he said he designed on 'a bit of cigarette paper.' The following year the Ferry yard completed the new 8m trawler *Lou Annie* for Stephen Crawford, who had been fishing for twenty-three years from the Ferry and has one of the fresh fish stalls. This was in the middle of national gloom resulting from the Credit Crunch and fishermens ever lasting discontentment with the EU's appallingly wasteful fish quota policy.

When I wrote a book about the River Thames I was amazed at how political it was, London people gauged time by which Government was in power. On the East Coast people more usually gauge time by the things that really matter, namely severe gales, high tides and the years when the fish stocks failed.

The labrador Belle on her morning mid-winter walk beside the River Deben with Shottisham Creek wall in the background. Sheep used to graze on the saltings along the estuaries.

People often look at the countryside and say 'time has stood still here,' but it never has, there has always been change. Peer back into the mists of time and you see that each generation has imposed a different shape on the landscape according to the needs and fashions of the time.

The medieval manors leased numerous tiny fields to tenants, but in the Elizabethan period small farms appeared and field boundaries began to be pulled out to make larger fields. Because crop failure meant starvation everyone looked at the 'waste,' heaths and saltings along the estuaries, and wondered how they could be brought into cultivation. The early villages in the Sandlings often lacked a definite centre. There was a manor house with its church nearby but houses were dotted around wherever a well could be sunk for water. The great nineteenth century estate owners started building houses in groups, usually centred on a pub and shop. But since World War II the Planning Authorities have insisted on having houses grouped together to form village centres.

Because the light sandy soil dried out in the summer the farmers needed grazing on the marshes, where the water table was high. The Anglo-Saxons might have walled off some small areas of marshes, but the larger areas needed considerable capital investment and organization that was undertaken by the medieval monastic orders. Grazing on the King's Marshes at Orford (which was then part of Sudbourne) was started in 1171 when 700 sheep and a boat to get them across the River Ore were purchased. This appeared to be a commercial venture intended to help support King Henry II's new castle in the new town of Orford.

The walling on the East Coast was on a par with building the pyramids; it was all done by hand. It must have been a daunting task for the men when they turned up with shovels and barrows, to throw up a dirt bank all the way up

The last bends on the River Blyth below Blythburgh road-bridge. This scene is the nightmare of the East Coast where tidal water has driven people and wildlife out.

The exposed posts were placed there in the eighteenth century when the walls were built. As the former river walls eroded away bird nesting sites and habitat were lost as the increased tidal water drags the soil out to sea. The loss of the river wall also made it difficult for boats to find their way up river. In about 2004 the River Blyth Navigation Association started putting navigation marks in the channel below Blythburgh road-bridge. Canoeing trips to Halesworth have also been undertaken to maintain the navigation.

from Orford to Sudbourne.

The wealth of Butley Priory came from the rent it received from its tenants. However the Butley records show that the monks found it hard to keep up with cost of maintaining river walls. After one disastrous flood, by a high tide, they wrote to the King for assistance. The King did not give them money but later, in 1478, Canon William, a Commissioner of Walls and Fosses was appointed to sort out the difficulties of landowners on the lower Deben and River Ore. The Commissioners, who had been long established, had the power to levy rates on landowners to maintain the walls. The Butley monks were very good at looking after their property and commandeering more and the Greenwell Estate still owns the bed of the Butley River.

The second burst of walling came in the Elizabethan era, when there was a tremendous hunger for land. There was a major change in the way land was cultivated. The Lord of the Manor had been renting out tiny plots of land and this system was replaced when landowners created farms with larger fields The land owners rented the land out to farmers who employed labourers. Many Suffolk half-timbered farmhouses were built at this time, and they had Georgian or early Victorian fronts added before the Repeal of the Corn Laws in the 1840s.

Defences against the sea always get a push forward when there is a positive Government in London. Henry VIII took the defences of the realm very seriously and he worried a great deal about the 'rage of the sea' flooding good productive land. In the 1520-30s Butley Priory had a massive project of walling off marshes in Bawdsey. People obviously knew that something important was happening and in 1528 Henry VIII's sister Mary and her husband the Duke of Suffolk were in a party that came to look at the amazing work of walling off the Hollesley and Alderton marshes.

Looking up the Butley River towards Chillesford Fleet. This was the 'Tiffin Station' at Gedgrave Cliff during the Alde and Ore Association's first walk from Orford to Chillesford, 2009.

In the 1540s the Duke of Norfolk had another 400 acres walled off at Hollesley. Gwen Dyke, who had access to documents in the Bawdsey Estate office before they were burnt, had seen a map of 1587 that showed that the Buckanay Marshes were still tidal right up to Bawdsey East Lane. Ships had been going up Hollesley Haven (Barthorp Creek), to a quay on the opposite side to the church, just below the road bridge, but eventually the haven silted up.

The sea suddenly reclaims its old territory about once a century. One wild night in 1953 the Coastguards rang up my grandfather, Morris Turner at Church Farm, Hollesley saying they had reports of flooding and advised him to get his cows off the marshes. In the dark in a full gale he went out on the marshes and got his herd back up to the buildings. At daylight, to his horror, the Floods had engulfed all the marshes. Even the gateposts were under the water. Shingle Street was cut off for several days and the Rev Will Groom rowed out with food and the post lady was rowed out to deliver letters. That's a proper postal service.

The Chillesford Fleet, on the Butley River, was walled off in about 1598. The 1953 Floods (said to have been a one in seven hundred years tide) 'over topped' the river wall here, but fortunately the wall had been repaired the previous year. This meant that there were no expensive breaks to repair, but the wall was strengthened at the back. On the Deben the marshes on either side of Bawdsey Fleet were walled off in two sections, the second enclosed Green Point marshes, leaving the Fleet as open water until the mid-Victorian period.

On the River Blyth walling didn't get going on a large scale until the eighteenth century. Posts were put in to hold the soil firm, and the labourers barrowed soil up to create a river wall. By 1770 they had enclosed 700 acres and there were five projects before 1845 when they had enclosed 2,704 acres (1094 hectares) or four and a half square miles of land. The

Tangham is sited at the head of the tiny Tang River. The original farm was probably here because ponds could be dug to provide drinking water, although sheep can live for long periods without drinking. The Tang runs down through the Scotland Fens, Boyton and into the Butley River, south of Barrow Hill.

Bulcamp marshes had been reclaimed in two projects, in 1770 and 1805. Walling was a skilled occupation because the mud had a habit of just sliding back where it had come from.

The medieval landowners were mostly looking to get a return from renting out grazing for sheep in the summer. By the eighteenth century the Suffolk marshes became very important for fattening cattle, brought down by drovers from Scotland for a big Fair at Melton and then when they were fat they were driven to the London markets.

In the great agricultural depression between 1870-1914 and again between 1921-29, many river walls were not maintained. In 1928 the wall just below Blythburgh Bridge broke and was not repaired so the marshes were left flooded. Lord Stradbroke employed six men to maintain his river walls on the Blyth, they had a boat to bring mud up to heighten the walls. On the Deben on a high tide the Hemley Hall marshes were flooded in about 1938 and

the Sutton Hoo marshes shortly afterwards after a bomb created Hackney Hole. But these walls were not repaired, even though the Government was reviving agriculture, ready for another European war, and this land is still flooded by the tide.

In World War II there were hardly enough men to work the farms let alone repair river walls. After the war there was a food shortage and every effort was made to bring land into cultivation. I remember a huge gang of Italian prisoners of war shovelling soil up on to the river wall at Peyton Hall, Ramsholt. It is not just high tides that flood low land, flooding is also caused by a lack of attention to river defences.

The marshes at Shottisham Creek were partly reclaimed; possibly even in the Anglo-Saxon period, but in the early nineteenth century, after the oyster fishery failed, the whole creek was walled off. In 1904 a young man, who was cycling back home along the footpath from Sutton, was thrown off his bicycle by the

Simon Read working on the River Deben Association's tidal deflexion walls on the Sutton saltings on the River Deben, 2009. These saltings were never successfully walled off and it was discovered that they were eroding away and losing an important habitat for young fish.

force of the river wall breaking behind him. His parents, the Butlers, heard the roar of the wall breaking at their cottage and rushed out on the marshes, but their son got home safely.

The 1904 high tide burst through Alderton beach and a barge was towed around from Ipswich and sunk in the gap. She is still there. By 1904 landowners thought that as they were paying rates to Government bodies to maintain the river walls they naturally thought that the Government should repair them. Sir Cuthbert Quilter refused to pay for the Shottisham Creek wall to be reinstated and the breach remained open for several years before it was closed.

The 1953 Flood tide went right up to Shottisham Mill again, closing the road. Mrs Lingley, an elderly lady living in the cottage near the Ford Hill, was rescued through the bedroom window and never went back in the house again. Geoffrey Ingram-Smith told me that their firm had the contract to close the Shottisham Creek gap. They rigged up a wire gantry to pick up silt mud from the 'cant' edge at the bottom of the tide range. They built two corrugated iron walls and filled the area between with mud, but just as they had filled the wall the first time the whole lot collapsed and they had to start again.

It was believed many river walls collapsed in the 1953 Flood because of the pressure of the water put on the wall. To overcome this walls were made higher and the main drainage ditch running behind the wall, the 'deft,' was moved further back. In spite of this massive construction on all the estuaries it had no long-term ill effect on the wildlife.

The huge cost of repairing the walls after the 1953 Floods did not seem to be a national problem. At the time the Prime Minster, Sir Winston Churchill, spoke on the BBC saying that the East Coast would be properly defended against the sea. Churchill's political career had

been devoted to protecting Britain. To him keeping the sea out was as important as keeping out Nazi Germany. Much of the coast would have been abandoned and simply vanished into the North Sea if the defences had not been repaired. It also gave the confidence to stay on the coast and redevelop everything from nature reserves to tourist activities, to say nothing of the tremendous amount of land protected for vital food production. The nation and the wild life got a very good reward for the money invested in sea and river defences.

Inland from the estuaries are the great Suffolk pine forests. A century before this area would have been open heath, totally different. In the medieval period the production of wool was a major economic earner. Because sheep can live without water for long periods they were taken up on to the open Sheep Walks (heaths). As agricultural knowledge improved in the nineteenth century sheep were grazed on

the saltings or heaths in the daytime and the flocks were driven back on to the fields at night so that their dung would give the soil nitrogen.

In the nineteenth century Tangham Farm and a few cottages stood alone in a vast open sheep walks straddling the Sandlings peninsula between the Deben and the Alde. Although the soil was very poor, Tangham Farm had been a going concern while sheep paid. A Victorian farmhouse had replaced the early Elizabethan house, but when wool began to be imported from Australia this sheep farm's usefulness ended. Lord Rendlesham, who owned much of the Sandlings heath, sought to find something profitable to do with this vast acreage. He was led to believe that lupins would grow on this soil at Tangham and lupins were drilled in the fields around the farm.

To the south of the Tangham Farm fields Lord Rendlesham started planting Tangham Forest, but some of this was burnt down

Sheep grazing on Tinker's Walks, Walberswick, 2008. In the interwar years the estate owners kept sheep grazing on the heaths to create good 'partridge ground.' In about 1975 the Nature Conservancy Council started grazing Tinker's Walks with sheep to help replace bracken with short turf to create bird habitat.

Newdelight Walks on the edge of Dunwich Forest have been reverting to forest in the many decades since they were grazed.

during World War I. Following this war Lord Rendlesham was extremly pleased to sell his barren heath to the newly formed Forestry Commission. During World War I the German and Allied armies had fought themselves to a standstill in the trench warfare in northern France, but in the North Atlantic the German submarines sank so many merchant ships that Britain was almost starved of resources to keep the war going.

The mining industry was almost brought to a stand still because pit props could not be imported.

The Government started the Forestry Commission so that the nation would never be starved of timber again and this proved vital during World War II. The 2,544 acre Tangham Forest was renamed Rendlesham Forest, although the locals still use the old name, and more land was bought to increase it to 3,958 acres. The 3,064 acre Tunstall Forest was planted up and with the 1,650 acre Dunwich Forest the Comission became the largest land owner on the Suffolk coast.

It takes about sixty years to produce a crop of pine in the Sandlings so that the trees cut down during World War II may have come from the original Tangham Forest. Photographs show young women in bare feet, 'Lumber Jills,' happily sawing up trees with no sign of safety guards.

Another World War II feature of Rendlesham Forest is the remains of FIDO fuel storage tanks. During World War II planes returning to Woodbridge airfield were often unable to see the runway through the fog. Petrol burners were put down on either side of the runway and when it was foggy these were lit to help the pilots guide the returning planes down. This worked very well, saved many lives, but burnt an astonishing 125,000 gallons of petrol per hour during wartime fuel shortages.

Over on the eastern side of Rendlesham

The by-road between Walberswick Lodge Road and the Five Cross Ways at Westleton. Many by-roads would have looked like this before the country roads were tarred.

Forest is the site of the UFO landing legend. Something undoubtedly happened on December 27 1960 when two USAF security patrolmen outside the East Gate of RAF Woodbridge Airfield saw unusual lights in the sky. As the Cold War was at its height these sighting were taken very seriously and the Deputy Base Commander, Lieutenant Colonel Charles Halt made a full investigation. The only evidence was some broken branches on the treetops. Halt believed that there really had been a UFO landing, but although it received international attention no evidence has ever been found to back this up.

The pine forest of the 'Sandlings Beat' covered some 10,000 acres and was originally intended to provide pit props for the East Midlands coal fields. This 'factory forest' was run from Tangham, a hamlet of thirteen houses in Rendlesham Forest. The shift from timber production towards leisure activities, mainly walking and camping and then horse riding, started in the 1970s. The public seem to find the sheer vast silent woodland very attractive.

At the same time the numbers of deer in Rendlesham and Tunstall Forests increased. Quite where they came from originally remains a mystery; most of the local deer were hunted to extinction in the early nineteenth century. The wild deer in East Suffolk appear to be the descendants of the fallow deer that jumped over the fences of Campsea Ash Park or the red deer that escaped from Helmingham Hall. Rendlesham also has muntjac and the Chinese water deer live in the woods of coastal villages, because they like reed beds. Most intriguing are the red deer that are just found in Dunwich Forest. These are larger than the Scottish red deer that have been reintroduced to the West Country and some believe they are 'Saxon' deer and might be the last survivors of the original native deer.

The deer numbers in the Sandlings shot up in the 1970s when autumn-sown cereals replaced varieties sown in the spring. In effect the farms, which provide most of the food for wildlife, became important winter grazing for deer. No one knows for sure how many deer are in the East Suffolk coastal area but it is not uncommon to see a herd of sixty deer on Hollesley Common. Far more than the area can support. The management policy in the Forestry is to keep a healthy population by culling about a third of the population. Most years the Forestry Commission cull and sell about 250 deer.

Change came to the great pine forests slowly, the last trees for pit props went away in the early 1980s and a few years later the empty space attracted the first New Age Travellers. It is believed that the first people living in old buses and vans in the Forestry were protesters to Sizewell B nuclear power station, but the numbers steadily grew. In our liberal society the law is very generous to anyone who chooses to live an alternative livestyle. Numerous attempts have been made to solve the problem by providing proper camping areas and clearing up the mess. However the nature of the travellers on heaths is anti-establishment and their groups are unable to agree representatives to reach a compromise.

Travellers also took advantage of the open spaces on Sutton and Upper Hollesley Common and established camps there. Sheep grazing on Hollesley Common finished in about 1936 and in 1988 the Hollesley Common Management Association was set up. In the 1990s sheep were re-introduced on Sutton Common, near Gobblecock Hall, for nature conservation. They didn't foresee that squatters would keep moving around the heaths and forests.

Beside the road leading to the Forestry Commission office at Tangham is a lone oak, planted, so a plaque said, by Lord Howe to commemorate the replanting of Rendlesham Forest after the Hurricane of 1987. There had been isolated incidents of high wind before, on November 18 1963 a sudden whirlwind struck Quay Street, Orford taking the roof off part of the 'Jolly Sailor,' but between 5-7am on October 16, 1987 a full blown Hurricane had roared up the East Coast. It was the most severe wind to hit England since the Great Storm of 1703. The miracle of the 1987 Hurricane was that no one was killed in Suffolk, because it took place while most people were still in bed. Had large numbers of people been driving or been outside there would have been a terrible loss of human life. Fallen trees closed nearly all the roads and the power lines were down in most villages. It was about a month before normal life resumed and far longer before trees were cleared from the fields.

Pat Mitchell was living in the Foresters Lodge at Tangham the night the Hurricane went through. Just before dawn, while gusts of up to 100mph went through there was so much noise from the wind buffeting the house that Pat and his wife had little idea what was happening outside. As dawn broke they saw complete devastation because in the space of about two and a half hours sixty per cent of the Corsican and Scots pine trees and Douglas fir in the Sandlings forests were levelled to the ground and became a huge jumble. Some sixty years of work in the forest was wiped out.

For the next three years woodcutters came down from Thetford Forest, in two coaches, and slowly cleared up the tangled mess. Some 450,000 tons of timber was saved and sold which was the equivalent of eleven years of harvesting the forest. The Forestry Commission had far more pine than the manufactures and house builders needed so thousands of tons were stored at Thetford where irrigation water from a lake was played on the bundles. Keeping the timber wet meant that eleven years later it could still be sold and it was as fresh as if it had just been cut down. The tops of the trees, which were bent, were sold for wood pulp, mostly to Gothenburg.

Since it was going to be another twenty-five years before even thinning Sandlings forests could start, a new management policy began to develop the forest for wildlife conservation. It was realized that the areas where trees had fallen provided a perfect habitat for woodlarks and nightjars so it was decided they should become the priority.

The Forestry Commission changes, like everything else. In 1967 Rendlesham employed thirty men, there were twenty-two men working in Tunstall and another twelve in Dunwich and there were often other workers in the areas of trees that had been sold standing. Forestry was labour intensive, as they used to have horses to drag trees out. The last time they used a horse was in Dunwich in 1990.

By 2009 all the work was done by contractors so that there were only four people permanently employed on the 10,000 acre 'Sandlings Beat,' a group of woodlands based at Tangham. Even the administration work has got simpler. In 1988 the Commission office at Tangham had its first word processor and in 1990 its first computer.

I don't know when the first computer was used in a work place in East Suffolk, but a very early one must have been in 1957, following a Ford scholarship trip by Frank Brown of Eastern Counties Farmers, to the United States. He found that all the American animal compounders were using computers to blend their products. On his return he had a computer installed in the ECF head office in Princes Street, Ipswich to regulate the animal 'feed' made at their Fore Street Mill, the site of which is under the University Campus Suffolk's Waterfront building that was opened in 2008. When the original ECF computer was installed it filled a whole room and most of us had never even heard of one. Certainly I hadn't and I used to cart animal feed stuff away from the Fore Street mill in a 7 ton petrol Bedford lorry. I was much more concerned as to whether the loaded Bedford would make it up the steep Back Hamlet hill with a heavy load and the accelerator flat on the floor. Soon after this I did hear of a computer being installed at British Sugar's Sproughton Road factory, again it was reported to fill a room. It was not until the 1980s that computers began to make a real impact and I was a bit behind the times when I started using one to write in 1987. I had difficulty in understanding it and remember a rather irritated young salesman telling me I was simply the wrong generation to use one. That was twenty-three years ago so goodness knows what I am now!

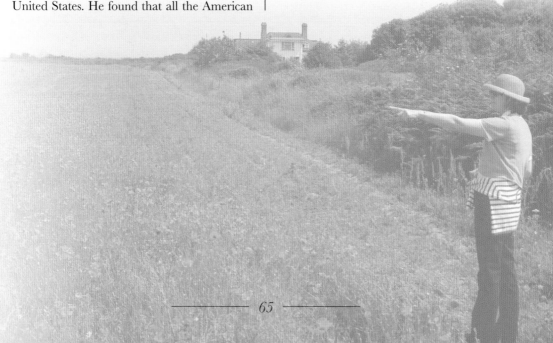

Chapter Five / THE GREAT ESTATES

Just after World War II, there was a tremendous drive to make Britain self sufficient in food. The Government policy was to end the reliance on imported food and farmers were encouraged to plough up 'waste' land. This led James Mann, who had bought the former 'Battle School' in Iken and Sudbourne to clear part of Sudbourne Great Wood. The bulldozers found a mantrap. This serious piece of eighteenth century ironwork was designed so that should a man step on the plate it would have sprung to and the iron teeth crushed his foot off. This anti-poacher device must have been intended to protect the sporting game of the great estates, in this case no doubt, Sudbourne Hall.

For centuries people who lived in the villages on the Suffolk coast very seldom owned any part of them. In the distant past villages were divided up between several landowners, mostly absentees, who relied on the rent, for their income. In times of high agricultural return they invested in new farmhouses, cottages and farm buildings. In periods of poor returns they did nothing. Pheasant and partridge shooting changed this, landowners wanted to own blocks of land so that they could 'preserve' the game. They did this with small armies of gamekeepers.

It was more or less open warfare between the men in the villages (I have never heard of a women poacher) and the gamekeepers employed by the great landowners. The battle of wits between the gamekeepers and poachers was at a very personal level as they all lived in the same village and had often grown up together.

In the medieval period the aristocracy favoured hunting deer as a leisure pursuit, but when firearms became general the landowners in East Anglia switched to shooting partridges, fast flying birds native to the area. The disadvantage with partridges was that even with careful game keeping it was difficult to create large numbers. Instead the pheasant became the game bird of choice for country sportsmen because they flew well over 'guns,' making a challenging target, and by keeping down 'vermin' that destroyed their eggs the numbers could be increased.

The drawback to the pheasant was that it was a rather showy bird and didn't have a have high level of self-protection. In fact it made life very easy for the poacher. As it got dark the pheasants would fly up into a low branch of a tree, to perch for the night, and would call out to each other. The poacher only had to listen quietly to know where the birds were roosting. Then, on a moonlit night all he had to do was walk around and reach up and take the birds off the branches. This method worked well for

Butley Abbey Farm is on the site of Butley Priory. The original Priory buildings covered two and a half acres and the Gatehouse still survives.

When the Marquis of Hertford bought Sudbourne Hall in 1784 the Elizabethan Hall was pulled down and he had a new brick mansion built. In 1953 this mansion was pulled down leaving the stable block. Behind the stable block, now converted to flats, are the former workshops and saw mill of the Sudbourne Estate. The nineteenth century estate owners backed up by their wealth from industry and ran their estates as self-contained kingdoms, not always as economic units.

a Sunday dinner, but for making money it had its limitations. Some birds perched on high branches, in which case a small shotgun was used. In both cases the gamekeeper was likely to hear the activity in his woods, but estates were often very large so that it was difficult for them to cover every wood. Sometime poachers would watch a keeper's cottage and see which way he set off on patrol and then go and raid the woods in the opposite direction. The keepers fought back by putting cords across the path so that in the dark the poacher walked into them and an alarm gun was set off. In Essex, gamekeepers loaded carriages with salt to fire at gypsies who were poaching.

One of the best money-making schemes for the poaching gangs was 'dragging' the fields in the autumn. After harvest the fields were covered in loose grain which was of great benefit to all wildlife and pheasants and partridges fed on this and then spent the night sleeping on the ground. The poaching gangs used to drag nets across the fields, a soundless method that caught everything. The keepers retaliated by 'bushing' the fields, cutting branches out of the hedges and sticking them up on the fields to foul the nets, although sometimes they turned up in the morning to discover both 'bushes' and the game had gone.

Even after mantraps were outlawed the poachers could, if caught, expect harsh treatment. Just firing a gun after dark could have led a man to be transported to Australia. In 1821 a man caught with five hares was fined £25, and when Sparrowhawk Smith of Blaxhall was caught setting traps at Ufford he was ordered to pay £5 to the poor of his parish. These were huge sums of money for ordinary working men to find. The early records of court fines do not mention pheasants; it was not until gamekeeping methods improved in the late Victorian period that they came to the fore.

The real victims of the poaching wars were the gamekeepers and their families. They led lonely lives in isolated cottages and were often ostracised by most of the village. A keeper on the Ashe High House Estate in the 1940s recalled that if he went into the 'Buck's Head' on a Saturday night for a drink most of the men in the room would stop talking and turn their backs on him. The keepers were not highly paid, they were on about the same rate as a head horseman, and if they didn't 'show enough birds' to their employer on a shoot day they could expect to be dismissed. Sometimes a disappointed landowner would sack a head keeper on the spot. The other victim was the cock pheasant, a

Woolverstone Hall was built in 1776 for a successful London property speculator.

truly handsome bird. In the Victorian period they were slaughtered in vast numbers and were seen as emblems of the rich aristocracy. Even now bird spotters seldom bother to mention pheasants, as if they are not really part of the countryside, yet rural East Suffolk was shaped for their benefit.

The sheer number of birds shot on the great estates was staggering. The Rendlesham Hall Estate covered some 10,800 acres; most of the Sandlings peninsula from Rendlesham to Bawdsey, in the 1912-13 season this estate shot a 'bag' of 15,651. To achieve this number

the estate had clamps of swedes put into a wood for hares and rabbits to feed on and then surrounded the wood and shot everything that was driven out. This figure was dwarfed by Elveden Estate, in West Suffolk, that had a total bag of 81,877 in 1885-6, of which 58,140 were rabbits. The landowning families, which have survived, are often embarrassed and amazed by the excesses of their ancestors.

The winner in the great shooting era was the wildlife in general because the estates had woods planted and the heaths were kept intact. The estates guarded the countryside from the

activities of men and that allowed every species to survive. Also shooting was a great form of employment in the countryside, every estate had a small army of keepers and on shoot days every available man or boy was hired as a 'brush' to walk through the woods and fields and scare the birds over the standing 'guns.' Both guns and brushes found it exciting when the birds broke cover and flew en masse over the guns. Even now, on a calm winter's day, the Suffolk countryside can sound like a battlefield. Shooting is still an important part of the rural life of East Suffolk.

The nineteenth century estate owners reshaped the Suffolk countryside to suit the habits of the pheasants. Pheasants love nesting and hiding in bracken and reeds and the Suffolk coast was divided by rivers, and as pheasants hated flying over open water they couldn't be lured over on to neighbouring estate, by careful feeding. The keepers, tactfully encouraged by their employers, put a lot of effort into 'drawing' pheasants and other game on to their 'beat' from rival estates. Shooting bred fierce local rivalry.

There was the great landowner who came

down to breakfast the morning after his wife had died and announced to his surprised family 'Your mother will be cremated.'

The eldest son plucked up courage to ask 'why is mother being cremated when we have always been buried.'

The Father roared, as if the question was stupid, 'there are partridges nesting in the graveyard!'

In the early nineteenth century the ownership of land was a profitable enterprise and the sporting possibilities a bonus, but after the Repeal of the Corn Laws wheat prices dropped and so did land rents. After this, land ownership was a privilege that had to be paid for. On the Suffolk coast successful men bought land for shooting, but also pumped huge fortunes into the villages they had bought.

Many estates had their own architectural style of housing and model farm buildings. Most of these displays of wealth were lavished on the prestige village in the centre of an estate,

and it is still just possible to pick out where one estate finished and another started. The Bawdsey Estate built Model cottage, the front being in the shape of an M, while the Orwell Park Estate cottage didn't have a front door. The landowner disliked seeing 'the women of the village idling away their time gossiping with their neighbours.'

The classical style, Woolverstone Hall, was built on the site of a former hall that overlooked the River Orwell. William Berners, a property developer who also owned Berners' Street, off Oxford Street in London had this Hall built in 1776. The Woolverstone Park Estate took in much of the land from the River Orwell towards the River Stour. Then there was Bawdsey Manor, a Victorian mansion on a cliff-top overlooking the sea that was the heart of an estate on the eastern shore of the River Deben. When Bawdsey Manor was sold in 1936 the owner drew out rough plans on a piece of paper and sent instructions to the agent to build him a

Cock pheasants, Kings of the Suffolk Coast, fighting over a hen pheasant.

new house at Methersgate Hall overlooking the River Deben. This estate didn't quite join up with the Red House estate in Hollesley. In 1885 the Red House estate became the Hollesley Bay Colony. Here young men were trained to go out into the British Empire and develop a rural economy. Further up the coast was the great Sudbourne Hall Estate that covered most of the land from the Butley River past Orford to Iken.

To the north of the River Alde was the 2,800 acre Black Heath Mansion Estate that took in the villages of Friston, Snape and the lost village of Hazelwood. This village, like so many Suffolk Sandlings parishes did not have a centre, but in 1853 102 people were living there and it is now part of Aldeburgh. The Ogilvies, who had made a fortune building railways in Scotland, sold up their estates north of the border and moved to Aldringham because the pheasant shooting on the Suffolk heaths was better. Their estate once covered seven miles of the coast between Thorpeness and Dunwich.

Then there was the Dunwich Hall estate which sold up just after World War II because the owners couldn't afford the cost of maintaining the big house and all the property. Even further north still was the Benacre Hall estate.

Inland there was Rendlesham Hall Estate and Ashe High House as well as many smaller estates. The Ashe High House, centre of the 2,350 acres Campsea Ash estate, was built in about 1585 and had Dutch crow-step gables, all the fashion at the time. This had been one of few East Suffolk country houses of great antiquity, but it was pulled down in 1953.

The Estates were completely self-contained kingdoms, usually run from an estate office. The agent was the most powerful man in the village with the head keeper being the second most powerful. The estates had their own mills, brickworks, sawmills and teams of builders. The true estate era finished with World War I so that Little Haddon Hall, built in 1914, and the Sutton Hoo House, never really had time

In the second half of the nineteenth century rich industrialists started to buy up Suffolk estates and build grand country houses and better cottages for their workers. Here at Bawdsey Hall are Victorian flint cottages that appear to have been built by the Tollemaches and a Model Cottage, with the fronts in the shape of an M, built about thirty years later by the Bawdsey Estate.

The Cat House on the Woolverstone Hall estate was built in the Regency period of local brick in a 'picturesque' style, so as not to clash with the 14th century church just inland. In Richard Cobbold's novel 'Margaret Catchpole' a white cat was placed in the window of the Cat House, at night, to warn smugglers that the Revenue men were in the area.

to develop into full-size estates. Walter Boynton, who had a wealthy wife, rented Melton Grange and bought up farms in Boyton and Butley. When wheat prices collapsed in 1921 his tenant farmers left, he took on farming the land himself and went bankrupt.

The Broxted House Estate in Sutton was a little different from the other estates because the Pauls continued to live in Ipswich in a large house on Constitution Hill so that they could be near their mills and maltings on Ipswich Dock. They bought the Sutton farms and Sutton Commons, mostly from Lord Rendlesham, so that they could entertain German malt buyers with a day's pheasant shooting. However it was not until the end of the twentieth century that any of the family lived permanently at Broxted House. This family also had another estate at Wherstead and in 2007 the family combined to open the Suffolk Food Hall to sell products from their farms.

The great landowners generally looked after their estates and that included keeping their

people happy. In the medieval period land was left for people to play Camp, a sort of football with a lot of violence and few rules, which often resulted in serious injuries and even deaths. In the nineteenth century the landowners encouraged cricket, a game they had learnt at Public Schools, and started to sponsor village cricket clubs.

In 1845 John George Sheppard was the owner of Ashe High House and he started a cricket club in the park. He even persuaded the famous cricketer I.Zingari to come down to play. In the 1930s Viscount Ullswater, speaker in the House of Commons, owned the estate.

As a child I used to climb over the fence, with my cousin Richard Turner, from Ashgreen Farm and explore the deserted gardens of Ashe High House. A large garden seat with a huge wooden back was supposed to be the stern galley of a ship that had sunk in the Battle of Sole Bay in 1672. This seat intrigued me, but it sounded too good to be true. The figurehead outside the 'Red Lion' at Martlesham is also

The 'hunt field' crossing the Dock Marshes, Ramsholt while the hounds pursue a dragged scent. There was deep enmity between the great pheasant shooting estates and the hunts until the law banning hunting with hounds was mooted. Then the estates opened up their land, out of solidarity, after the season for pheasant shooting ended.

thought by many to have come off a ship in the battle of Sole Bay between the combined English and French fleets against the Dutch. A battle watched for some fourteen hours by crowds standing on the cliffs at Southwold.

After World War II the old style of country estates, with the all-powerful Lord of the Manor in his grand house, was swept away. Since that way of life seemed gone forever Ashe High House was pulled down. The farms of this estate were sold to Sir Peter Greenwell of Butley Abbey who was extending his farm estate. The Campsea Ash cricket club lost its cricket pitch and the team moved to Woodbridge School and became The Deben Valley club. Fifty-five years later a cricket club restarted in Ashe Park.

The Sudbourne Hall Cricket Club was started by Lyon when he owned the hall, his two sons, B.H.Lyon, and, M.D.Lyon, were both county cricket players. The cricket pitch was in the Hall's grounds and local unemployed men were hired to build a pavilion. Orford was very much an estate town, the sailing club originally

being the Sudbourne Hall's boat house. They also had a bowls club behind the 'King's Head'. In the past most country pubs had a small meadow where visitors could leave their horses and these became an ideal site for a bowling ground, with players having a drink in the pub after the game. In the 1980s, when the property boom started in East Suffolk, brewers realised that these little meadows had become good earners as house sites.

The Berners had a cricket ground, with its thatched pavilion, in Woolverstone Park. The Berners also had their own otter hunting pack, kept in kennels just outside the park gates. In 1937 the Berners sold up and moved inland to be near fox hunting country, but the village cricket club continued until about 1988 when the Ipswich High School bought the Hall.

Another estate also started the cricket club, this time at Bawdsey, The story here is that the new estate owner, a successful London stockbroker, applied to join the Cricket Club at Lord's, but was not elected. He was less than

The Butley River with George Watson's longboat, near the Hut. In 1927 an old harness room from the Sudbourne Hall Estate was placed here as a bathing hut. This was for Alistair Watson's Chillesford Lodge Estate, part of the old Sudbourne Hall Estate.

In 1911 John Lomax, a successful timber importer, built the Edwardian country house at Sutton Hoo. Lomax died in 1916 and in 1926 the house and 500 acre estate was sold to the Prettys. At some point the house was pebble-dashed.

pleased with this decision and to keep his end up he decided to create a cricket pitch larger that the one at Lord's. The area in front of Bawdsey Manor was levelled and the Jordan, a former creek from the River Deben mouth that had been used for punting, was partly filled in and a cricket pitch created.

In 1936 the Government bought Bawdsey Manor to develop radar on high coastal ground. The Bawdsey Cricket Club was moved to a new Recreation Ground, referred to as 'the Rec,' behind Bawdsey Street, (once called The Thoroughfare). Being an Estate team, the practice of asking the Estate Office to supply new balls and bats continued. However, in 1953 the Estate was sold and the Cricket Club nearly folded because people in the village just could not understand that they had to buy their own equipment.

Rendlesham Hall was the first of the great estates to break up. In the early 1900s Bawdsey Estate's agent was travelling up to the Houses of Parliament for meetings with Lord Rendlesham to reach agreement about purchasing more land to extend the Bawdsey Estate. Rendlesham, or likely his agent, had tried to develop his open heath for growing lupins. Tangham Farm was in the middle of the heath and a lupin growing project was started here to improve the fertility of the soil. Cottages were built for more workers, and lupins must have been grown here, and at Wantisden Hall, because barges used to come to Boyton Dock to load lupins to go to Belgium for making dye, but this project petered out. During World War II Wantisden, a parish of scattered houses where eighty people had lived in 1922, more or less vanished under the runways of the USAF Air Base at Bentwaters, with the tiny church of St John's just beside the perimeter fence.

A re-enactment play was held at Sutton Hoo for the National Trust in 2009, to celebrate the seventieth anniversary of the Sutton Hoo dig, when Basil Brown discovered the famous Anglo-Saxon ship burial in 1939. Here 'Basil Brown' is seen touching his cap to 'Mrs Pretty.'

The Rendlesham Estate also started planting up trees on the former sheep walks and created Tangham Forest, but fire destroyed some of the forest in about 1917. In 1922 the Government bought Tangham so that the new Forestry Commission could plant trees and continued buying land from the Sutton Hoo estate to enlarge the new pine forests. During World War I the mining industry was almost brought to a stand still because pit props could not be imported. To prevent this happening again the Forestry Commission planted up vast acres of poor land throughout the British Isles.

In the 1930s each village had at least five or six independent farmers, but after World War II the pattern of arable land occupation changed. First, the old estates were squeezed very hard by taxation and then the 'economy of scale' was necessary to pay for the huge new machines needed to compete with imported food. The older estates, mostly greatly reduced in size, no longer rented out their farms, but began to take them 'in hand' and farm them as 'estate farms.' Some farming families also swallowed up the land around them to create 'super farms' extending over several parishes. As the returns from agriculture are usually fairly small, these new super farms were able to expand because they were not footing the bills of the huge cost of maintaining all the workers' cottages, which had put severe strain on the old estates.

The march towards large agricultural units had been going on since the Enclosure Acts of the eighteenth century. The only really serious attempt to halt this economic situation was the Liberal Party's 'one acre and cow' policy of the late nineteenth century. The agricultural depressions of the late Victorian era and again the slump in the inter-war years, both caused by the high value of the pound making imported

Deer on farmland near Bank's Grave Corner, Alderton in January 2009.

food cheaper, had created terrible rural poverty.

The Liberal's Smallholding Acts obliged County Councils to establish smallholdings. This was a very different form of land ownership and started in East Suffolk in 1909 with the County Council creating eighty-three smallholdings. After World War I the 'Land Fit for Heroes' saw another burst of land purchased and in 1936, when a 337 acre farm was purchased at Newbourne, the prime object was to provide work for unemployed miners. Basically Suffolk was being used to try and solve problems in other parts of the country. A theme that often appears in the county's history.

The forty-eight small-holdings at Newbourne were gradually taken over by local people, but were administered by the Land Settlement Association, a Government controlled body. The Land Settlements were run rather like a Soviet Co-operative farm in that tenants were not allowed to buy or sell anything, they were not even allowed to have bank accounts, and everything had to be done by the Management. The tenants, on 3-10 acre holdings, were only allowed to have pigs and chicken, but later this was changed so that they could buy glass-houses, but could only produce lettuces and tomatoes which all went to the London whole sale markets.

The Land Settlement became a huge costly bureaucracy, run from Cromwell Street in London, and suddenly in 1982 the Government announced that it was winding the scheme up, and offering to sell the tenants their holdings. Many, who had never really run their own business left, and the remaining holdings have, over the years, been bought up by people looking for a house in the country with a piece of land.

By 2009 only a few former Land Settlement holdings were in business growing some vegetables to retail in their farm shops. There were also three garden centres and one of these is Mervyn and Susan Spindler's Crystal Gardens holding that kept up the supermarket bean contract until it was cancelled in about 2002, and they then concentrated on producing bedding plants and flowers to sell direct to the public.

Mervyn and Susan Spindler's Crystal Gardens glass-house on the former Newbourne Land Settlement Estate.

Smallholdings provided a small answer to a larger problem, rather like organic farming that was promoted in the 1990s, offering a way for small-scale food producers to stay in business. A helping hand up the ladder, but not a solution to providing a long-term home produced food policy. The real solution to agriculture's future on the Suffolk coast came by linking the area's climatic advantage. It has an early growing season, and with irrigation has turned into a major vegetable growing area.

Birds, it seems, have long played a major part in shaping the Suffolk coastal countryside. In the nineteenth and part of the early twentieth century, shooting pheasant and partridge became a major obsession of the landowners in most villages. On the coast there was a small-scale occupation selling birds' eggs to the London market that had been gathered on the shingle. A shift in emphasis came when Richard Pinney pointed out to a keen 'birder' friend that avocets were nesting on the River Ore, after a break of about a century. The rest, as they say, is history. The Royal Society for the Protection

of Birds purchased Havergate Island in 1948 and this became a safe haven for avocets to re-establish themselves in England.

The public really enjoy watching wading birds in marshland on the coast and to cater for this demand more land has been acquired. By the beginning of the twenty-first century conservation groups had bought much of the county's coastal land, between Walberswick and Hollesley. In fact there is more wildlife habitat, if the pine forests and considerable amount of conservation projects in private ownership are included, on the Suffolk coast and Sandlings than there has been since the early medieval period. The new conservation landowners have remodelled the countryside, just as their predecessors did, to suit the requirements of specific birds but their attitude to the land is totally different. The old landowners fought to make sure that their land didn't go into the sea or become tidal waters, while the conservation groups actively discourage protection against erosion. As the land is collectively owned no one worries about its loss.

The stylised bird lands on the Suffolk coast just can't be replaced, if lost to the sea, without considerable loss of habit for other species, including humans. By and large, the Suffolk coast is a good place for birds, and bird watchers for the time being. To stand on the National Trust's Dunwich Common, on a still day, and listen to the bird song coming up from the RSPB's Minsmere Level or to watch a marsh harrier glide above the reeds on the Dingle Marshes touches something deep in most people.

A party of French school children near the Coastguard Cottages on the National Trust's Dunwich Common. The great shooting estates used to carefully record how many 'birds' (pheasants and partridges) were shot each season, while the conservation bodies carefully analyse the number of paying visitors that come to look at the variety of birds.

The view over the RSPB's reserve at Minsmere, from the National Trust's Dunwich Common.

We roped down the last trailer-load of wheat 'shuffs' (sheaves) ready for the short journey back to the farm 'stack yard.' This was in 1953 and we all leaned on our pitch-forks and surveyed the empty harvest field with the air of men who had done a job well and were proud of it. It was time for the young members of the harvest gang to keep very respectfully quiet while the old men reminisced about the harvests they had known.

Arthur Potter, who had started in Butley in the 1930s, remembered that the old men used to decorate the last loaded wagon and the Suffolk horses with wild flowers and branches, ready for the journey back to the stack yard. The last load of the cereal harvest was a great occasion in the rural year; all was safely gathered in. The hard dirty work of the winter threshing never raised the same level of excitement.

Walter Burch reminded us, many times, that in his youth the farmer bought the beer and the more they drank, the harder they worked. When the farmer wanted the work speeded up he sent a bottle of gin to spice up the beer.

However, too much beer, and they drank a lot, was counter productive. The men lost interest in the work, or perhaps were exhausted after weeks of toil, threw down their scythes and pitchforks and started to drink seriously. There were tales of a 'harvest company' in Alderton getting so drunk that they had races rolling down the Mount. Charlie Malster, who started work in the 1920s, remembered a gang scything peas in Ramsholt on piecework. The first day they worked like mad and earned well above their normal wages. The second day they sat in the hedge drinking, Charlie and the other boys spent all day running backwards and forwards to the 'Arms' getting more beer. He was still angry about his wasted day, 'why did those silly old men do that!'

There was even more anger left over from the days of child labour. How in the 1890s girls as young as ten were paid six pence a week, a shilling if they worked all seven days, to lead the Suffolk horses pulling the wagons between the fields and stackyards. The Suffolks were so strong that they could lift the girls off the ground, and they had to hang on tightly to prevent falling and going under the wagon

A view across the reed beds towards Butley Mill at the head of the Butley River. By having ownership of the mills, the medieval landowners controlled the villages.

wheels. 'That was never right' thundered the farmer who remembered this.

It was poverty that allowed child labour, the Church of England tried to help out. In Alderton the Vicar used to send his gardener round every Saturday morning to give soup to the poorer families. They stood more chance of getting extra soup if they had been to church the week before.

There had always been poverty in the villages, but when there was a poor growing season it was even worse. There was, when I was young, a memory passed down about the 'Hungry Forties' (1840s). Women used to go 'gleaning' after harvest, picking up the corn ears left lying on the field for 'chicken grub.' Back in the 1840s gleaning ears were actually used to feed the families. One family recalled how a boy had bread made from gleaned wheat and one day he exchanged his wheat bread for barley bread with the boy next door. He so disliked the barley bread that he didn't do that again.

In 1879 there was a very wet summer and much of the harvest was lost. Richard Rope at Sudbourne Lodge recorded that his wheat shuffs lay rotting in the fields as it kept raining. At Framlingham there were floods on the River Alde and people had to get to the station by boat. Rope finally finished his harvest on September 17 and since the roads were flooded he had to wait until the end of the month before his bullocks could be driven back from his Leiston marshes.

The bad harvest of 1879 was the start of the farming slump that lasted until 1914. Since cereal growing was the prime employment in lowland Britain, this led to terrible hardship. Food was being imported from the new colonies and the United States. This suited the population in the towns and the landowners, who invested in the British Empire, used the returns to develop their shooting estates.

The agricultural slump ended when the German submarines cut Britain off from a source of cheap imported food during World War I. Home-grown cereal prices shot up until 1921 when the merchant fleets had recovered enough to begin shipping foreign food in again. In East Suffolk many fields and

Hogweed near Thorpeness mill. The 1803 Thorpeness post mill was used to grind corn at Aldringham until 1923. This mill was moved to Thorpeness to pump water up to the 'House in the Clouds' by the Ogilvie Estate.

Red Polls, and some crossbred cattle on Moor's Farm, Hollesley. The red native cattle of southern England don't have horns and are part of the Suffolk Trinity that include the Suffolk Sheep and the Suffolk Horse. Some people believe that Red Polls descend from the cattle that the Anglo-Saxons brought in from Northern Germany.

farms were abandoned in the 1920-30s, while ships brought grain in to Ipswich Dock from Australia. Landowners sometimes leased land out rent free just to keep it in cultivation. This was cheaper than farming it at a loss.

In World War II Hitler's submarine campaign again sent merchant ships loaded with grain to the bottom of the sea. Starving Britain into submission came very close to being achieved in two World Wars. The politicians thought they had had enough of shortages and the Agricultural Act of 1947 set in motions policies to keep up the home production of food. The European mainland had suffered actual starvation during and just after World War II and the memory of food shortages here was even stronger than in Britain. The European Union carried on supporting food production, which was highly successful in Britain and Europe, so the shops and supermarkets were always full of food that people could afford.

Market forces divided agriculture into two types of farming enterprises. In Suffolk the continual development of very large machines in the 1990s allowed 'super farms' to cover several villages, whereas 'organic' foods allowed a few smaller specialized farms to continue. This catered for two markets the supermarkets wanted food as cheaply as possible, and put great pressure on farming enterprises to force prices down while the organic farms mainly supplied the farm shops.

This change in marketing was happening in 1995 when Howell Jenkins at Five Winds Farm, Bromeswell decided to give up pig production and concentrate more on butchery. Supplying local restaurants and schools proved to be popular and the business expanded. In 1998 the lease of Melton Station was taken on and Five Winds Farm Shop was opened.

The next step at Five Winds Farm was to have a smokehouse using smouldering oak chippings to add subtle flavours to the meat,

Tracy Pettit with the Suffolk mare Colony Gigi and her four-day old filly foal, at the Suffolk Punch Trust's Sink Farm, Hollesley, 2009. This farm was part of the Barthorp family's Hollesley Bay Estate that was formed when the Barthorp family bought land here between 1759 and 1805. This land has had a long association with the Suffolk horse. The Barthorps were some of the leading breeders on the 'Sands' who helped to develop the Suffolk horse, but in 1886 they turned their estate into the Colonial College to train young men to go out and farm in the British Empire. The Colonial College was taken over by the Receivers in 1903, but subsequent owners retained the Suffolk Horse Stud. When the Prison Service bought the Hollesley land in 1938 they kept the farm horses so that the Borstal boys could work the land. Since the Suffolk horse has become a rare breed the Suffolk Punch Trust was formed and Sink Farm, Hollesley became their base in 2006.

British carthorses existed in the 1500s but Suffolk has always been a progressive county and abandoned ploughing with oxen early on. The Suffolk horse is the oldest breed and all the pedigree Suffolk horses descend from one stallion, Crisp's horse, of Ufford, which was born in 1768. There are seven different shades of the 'chestnut' coloured Suffolk horses. In the past this colour was referred to as being 'sorrel.'

The Granary, with a cart lodge below, near St Peter's Church, Chillesford appears to have been built by the Sudbourne Estate. Farm granaries were always built within clear sight of the farmhouses so that the doors could be watched to prevent thieves.

duck, chicken and fish by 'cold smoking.' The two smoke houses at Orford use a 'hot smoking' system that actually heats and flavours the fish for preservation.

In the Sandlings the old farmhouses and cottages have large chimneys where meat used to be hung on iron hooks to catch the smoke and help preserve it. One of the reasons that so many hedgerows survived was that they provided fuel for household fires. The women of the villages used to go out in the afternoons looking for branches which had fallen down, and. in some cases encouraged them to fall down, to provide wood for the fires under their washing coppers. Most houses were fitted with coal-burning ranges in the nineteenth century for cooking and heating.

One of the important businesses in the countryside was the corn and coal merchant which bought the farmer's grain and retailed coal. From the medieval period to the 1960s great fleets of colliers brought coal from the North East down to ports of the South East. In 1507 colliers were bringing coal from Newcastle to Iken Cliff and in the nineteenth century the Ropes continued with this trade. For grain they had a granary at Iken Cliff, at the bottom of the lane leading down past the 'Anchor' pub, in the bend of the River Alde so that their schooners could get alongside. This granary was abandoned when Newson Garrett took the trade up to his coal yards at Snape Maltings.

The Southwold schooner, *Hearts of Oak*, discharged coal into horse tumbrels on the open beach at Dunwich every summer between 1860-70. In the Victorian period

Howell Jenkins at Five Winds Farm smoke house, Bromeswell where streaky and back bacon were being smoked, 2009. Slightly away from the smoke house and butchery, at Five Winds Farm, is Howell and Johanna Jenkins' other enterprise, the Five Winds Farm Stud, where they breed Welsh cobs for riding and carriage driving. Howell is very proud of being the fourth generation to breed Welsh cobs.

the Southwold schooner *Woodland Lass* traded regularly up to Blythburgh. She brought coal in from Hartlepool and Baltic timber for Bickers at Wangford. The schooners couldn't get up the last few bends of the Blyth below the road bridge so they discharged at a quay out on the marshes where the river was still just wide enough for them to turn round. After the *Woodland Lass* was wrecked at Sizewell Sluice in the 1880s sailing barges came up to Blythburgh with stone for road making. The last barge up here appears to have been one sailed for pleasure in 1931.

Early Victorian schooners, tubby little ships with deep draft, took coal to Boyton Dock and sailing barges continued into the 1920s. Minter, the Boyton farmer and coal merchant, built the brick warehouse on the Dock in about 1900

and there was another farm wharf at Boyton on the River Ore. At Bawdsey coal was offloaded into a small horse-drawn barge and towed up Bawdsey Fleet to supply Thomas Garrod's brick and tile 'kell' (kiln) and Alderton village. A boy who used to ride on the horse's back until about 1860 was still alive in 1940 when he was the Bawdsey church warden. The whole Fleet silted up and it was difficult to believe that even a small barge could ever have got up there. The barge, according to local memory, eventually sank in one of the Alderton Hall marshes.

At Ramsholt Dock coal was stored in the open, in what is now the dinghy park, and then taken up to a coal yard at Alderton windmill. Captain Robert Skinner's barges called with part cargoes at Ramsholt and he retailed some coal straight to the local people. The farmers

Lady Caroline Cranbrook showing Prince Charles and the Duchess of Cornwall Bramfield Meats stall at the Snape Farmers Market, 2008. Lady Caroline Cranbrook campaigned to prevent a superstore being opened in the Saxmundham area. It is believed that this has kept many small food producers in business.

sent tumbrels for their winter supply while the cottagers often went with wheelbarrows.

Bawdsey Manor, the grand house overlooking the entrance of the Deben, had three barge loads of coke every year, about 240 tons, to fuel the fires in the big house and its greenhouses. These barges came into a dock by the quay above the ferry landing, which has now silted up. Methersgate Dock had a brick coal store and George Skinner told me that he once took the boomie barge *Lord Alcester* up to Robert Skinner's coal yard at the Jetty, Woodbridge with 290 tons of coal.

In the nineteenth century when the 64ft schooner *English Rose*, owned by George Disbury of Boyton, traded to the coal yard at the Ferry Dock it sometimes took sixteen men on her windlass to drag her through the mud to reach the end of the Ferry Quay. When she was bound for the Lime Kiln Yard, around the next bend, about 30 tons had to be taken out of her at Kyson into two small barges that were rowed. Eastern Counties Farmers took over the Ferry Dock and warehouses and had coal delivered by rail. The old coal yard became Frank Knights Shipwrights between 1947-2001.

When I was writing *Up The River Deben* Mel Skeet pointed out that he had moved a post in the channel that was used to haul barges up to the Dock at Melton. When Simon Read constructed the RDA tidal deflector on the Sutton Shore saltings in 2009 he found the remains of another post near the pre-1876 ferry landing hard opposite the Tide Mill. I looked more closely at the river and realised there had been series of posts between the Jetty, at Everson's, up past the Hackney Hole bends to Wilford Bridge. The Ipswich barge skipper Harold Smy, who had been on his father's

A 'tug of war' between the Locals and the Eastern European fieldworkers at the Ramsholt Fete in 2008. The Eastern Europeans won.

barge *Landfield* in the ballast trade to Wilford Bridge in the 1920s, said that 'it was easy to get up there, there were good pilots there.'

As Melton Dock was built in about 1793 and the Wilford Bridge wharf in 1840 these posts might pre-date the flat-bottomed spritsail barge, which were reasonably good to handle in a shallow narrow channel. The deep draft sloops and schooners, which came before barges, must have been very difficult to control in the narrow rivers so presumably these posts were put in for their benefit. This was fairly unique to the Deben, the only other hauling posts I know of are on the River Crouch up to Battlebridge, and they were on the top of the river wall.

The coal trade on the River Orwell was slightly different to the smaller rivers as steamers sometimes brought coal south and then smaller barges took it round to the farm 'docks' on the Orwell and Stour. There was a wooden barn at the head of Levington Creek and another wharf further down. In about 1910, when there was barge traffic on every creek wharf, there were sometimes three barges discharging in Levington Creek at the same time.

Some coal was brought direct to the Orwell from the north of England in boomie barges. The *Sussex Belle* brought coal to the Cat House for Berner's Woolverstone Hall. The hard at Pin Mill was enlarged, no doubt with shingle from Landguard Point, and renamed the Jubilee Hard, presumably after Queen Victoria's Diamond Jubilee in 1897. Edward Graham built up a small fleet of barges supplying Pin Mill and other small ports. Graham's *Sussex Belle*, skippered by John Ruffles, brought coal regularly from Keadby to Pin Mill right up until 1927, when she was driven ashore and wrecked at Great Yarmouth while on passage with coal from Keadby to Orford.

The strangest work Ruffles did with the *Sussex Belle* was to put a post in the sea off Bawdsey Manor for target practice. During the 1920s this post became known as The Monument because in the summer visitors used to ask the Felixstowe Ferry fishermen why the post was there. 'It's Nelson's Monument' the fishermen used to say with a glint in their eyes.

In the Victorian period sea transport remained cheaper than the railways, but the railway companies gradually improved their freight services and coal merchants relocated from the quaysides into the railway goods yards. The last of the small Suffolk ports to have coal brought in by sea was Orford, which was a long way from a station. Here, barges and small coasters brought in coal from the Humber during the summer until 1939. They filled up the brick warehouse on the quay and in the winter the coal was sold around the villages.

Steam coasters continued bringing coal to Ipswich and here the largest coal merchant was Mellonie on Neptune Quay in the Wet Dock.

After the Mellonies gave up, coal was still being brought in by sea to the Gas Works. This was down towards the dock gates and was referred to as being a 'foul place' by the shipping people because of the smell. The Gas Works had a ship with coal from Goole every other day until it closed in 1974. The Cliff Quay Power Station at Ipswich also consumed vast amounts of coal after being opened in 1950. The power station had a ship every day discharging about 4,500 tons of coal. This coal was stored on the quayside and often ignited and started to burn.

A fleet of colliers supplied Cliff Quay Power Station with coal from Blyth. These smart oil-fired steamers were very quiet running and for decades ploughed at 9 knots north and back south at 8 knots with coal. When the power station closed in 1982 the colliers *Cliff Quay* and two other CGB steamers were sold. They had been the last British cargo steam-driven ships.

Looking up the River Deben past the wreck of the barge *Westall* towards the old barge wharf at Wilford Bridge. The dot in the water near the *Westall* appears to be the stump of one of the hauling posts originally used to haul sailing craft up river. The tradition is that there were stepping-stones at Wilford (the name means Willow Ford) before the first wooden bridge was built in about 1530. This bridge was replaced with a hump-backed bridge in 1764 and this was replaced in 1939 with the present bridge.

The Blaxhall 'Ship' was named after the 'ships' (sheep) that once grazed the Heath. 'Houses where they sing' are the Butley 'Oyster', the Blaxhall 'Ship,' Eastbridge ' Eel's Foot' and inland, the Stradbrook 'Queen's Head.'

A dulcimer, an instrument often associated with East Anglia, being played aboard the Dutch ketch *Albatros*.

The sounds of the east coast are many and varied, the crash of the waves on the beaches or roar of wind in the treetops are perhaps the most outstanding. The music made by people here is just as varied. In the past, in puritan Suffolk, singing outside churches and chapels was not looked on as being desirable, but it went on all the same. People learnt the songs that had never been written down and passed on the steps of the dances. Most of the songs were about murder, sex, drinking and death. Sex was often heavily disguised and often wrapped up in heavy sentiment. These were the strong emotions that touched everyday life. Each song belonged to its singer and they had their own words that often changed as they passed on to a new singer. Most of the singing was in the pubs, although there was a tradition in East Suffolk that anyone with a good voice was expected to stand up and sing at a wedding feast.

The collecting and recording of folk songs started in the late Victorian period, particularly in Germany, a new country searching for a national identity. In Britain it was realised that we also had a strong tradition of folk music and people began going out and making written records.

Many classically trained composers became heavily influenced by folk music. Much of the music composed by Roger Quilter of Bawdsey Manor had its roots in folk music. In 1910 Ralph Vaughan Williams and George Butterworth arrived by train from London, with their bicycles, to make written records of folk songs in Southwold. The first evening they made records of eleven songs sung by William, Robert and Ben Hurr. The Hurrs were fishermen who worked some of the longshore boats then kept on the beach in front of Southwold.

It was very unusual at the time for upper class people like Vaughan Williams to go into the pubs with ordinary working men. However Vaughan Williams sat in the pubs and wrote down the songs as they were sung, although a century later his notes are often difficult to

Folk singing at the Stradbrook 'Queen's Head,' 2005.

follow. Butterworth was killed in World War I, but Vaughan Williams went on collecting folk songs as well as composing classical music. He recorded about 790 different songs in southern England and quite a few were from Suffolk. He believed that the tunes were very old indeed and the songs were often written to record a local event. The songs were sung as a way of passing on news, rather like a tabloid newspaper. At Shadingfield Williams recorded a song about the infamous murder of Maria Marten at the Red Barn in 1827. Another song he recorded at Southwold he believed dated back to the sixteenth century. The countryside, with its fixed population, had a very long memory.

The influence of folk music was on the decline when Benjamin Britten was a young man in the 1930s, but his first major work, 'Peter Grimes,' drew on a very English story. It is based on Crabb's poem of an Aldeburgh fisherman who treats the boys in his care very brutally. 'Peter Grimes' is now regarded as being the foremost British opera and its success has had a major effect on Aldeburgh. Even if Britten had never written a note, once the car became the leading form of transport, the London weekend influence would have extended into Suffolk, but estate agents claim that the rise of house prices in Aldeburgh was directly related to the growth of power and influence of the Aldeburgh Music Festival.

The Suffolk coast connection to pop music is not strong, but one event that changed the course of sound radio did take place here. In March 1964 I was told that the 'pirate radio' ship Radio Caroline was anchored off Bawdsey, broadcasting pop music. This was copying the success of Radio Veronica, which was broadcasting to The Netherlands from just outside her territorial waters. A few weeks later we sailed out around Radio Caroline, the former 763 ton passenger ferry *Frederica*, and one of the disc jockeys, I think Simon Dee, came out on deck and asked if we would like a record played. Next morning Radio Caroline played Francois Hardy's 'We Are Only Good

Brian Foster singing at the Ramsholt 'Arms.'

Friends' 'for the little boat *Sea Fever* that sailed around us yesterday.'

It was all very friendly and many of our generation heard it, we were all listening to pop music that the BBC didn't play. Other pirate radio stations appeared, anchored to the south. By the end of the year we had Radio Caroline, Radio City, Radio Victor and Radio London. There was tremendous competition, and on one occasion there was a gunfight between rival stations on the towers. By 1966, Radio Caroline South, Radio London, Radio City, Radio 390, Radio Britain and Radio England were operating in the Thames Estuary, with varying degrees of success. Once we sailed past four of them anchored off Walton Naze and sullen looking men on each one came on deck to watch us closely in case we tried to board them.

Towards the end of the pirate radio era the Rough Tower was occupied. Just off the coast at Felixstowe this tower had been one of a series of anti-aircraft gun platforms that Churchill had ordered to be built in the Thames Estuary. This platform became occupied by Roy Bates of Southend, and he declared that the Rough Tower was an independent state called 'Sealand.' Many years ago we sailed around the Rough Tower in *L'Atalanta* and Roy Bates came out and gave us a friendly wave. Even though it is beside one of the world's busiest shipping lanes it must be a lonely life on the Tower. The only time that the effect of 'Peter Grimes,' and Pirate Radio, came slightly together was the showing of Richard Curtis' film 'The Boat That Rocked' in Aldeburgh Cinema. This cinema was opened in 1919, but in 1965 the owner died and it was set to close. A group that included Benjamin Britten and Peter Pears bought the cinema. They wanted the building as offices for Aldeburgh Festival, but they kept the cinema open until the Festival bought the former East Suffolk Hotel, on the High Street. At this point Lettie Gifford, a diplomat's wife and one of the shareholders, sold her boat and spent the rest of life working for free, with three very loyal staff, to keep the cinema open. Once when we went there Lettie appeared in an interval with free cups of tea. In the end Lettie was given the MBE and Aldeburgh kept its cinema.

Every generation changes Suffolk a little bit, for better or worse, and the major changes have resulted from upheavals in Western Europe. The arrival of the Anglo-Saxons and the Vikings, then the Norman invasion created the basic layout. Wars with France and then two World Wars with Germany left more changes. World War II saw the United States Air Force building 'aerodromes' on a massive scale in southern England. After a brief period the United States Air Force was back again for the Cold War to deter the Soviet Union from extending its empire into Western Europe. The USAF personnel were living in almost every town and most of the villages in the Sandlings. In the last decades the USAF created all the facilities, such as shopping centres that only took dollars, on their Bases. The Americans left behind their major Air Bases at Bentwaters and Woodbridge (Sutton Heath) and the unsuccessful Cobra Mist early warning station on Lantern Marshes on Orfordness. Surprisingly after about fifty years of American presence very little long-term impact was made on Suffolk life, apart from local girls marrying servicemen. Many local families now have relatives in the United States. The next 'invasion' has been new residents moving into the area from other parts of the United Kingdom. This has made far more impact than the US Air Force. The growth of tourism has brought visitors from the rest of England and often far beyond. Although the Suffolk coast can give the impression of tranquillity it is an area of constant change.

Radio Essex. a former Trinity House lightship, off Shotley. This vessel was used when the film 'The Boat that Rocked' was made.

The Aldeburgh Cinema.

FELIXSTOWE

Landguard Fort sits guarding the entrance to Harwich Harbour. In the numerous wars with our European neighbours this was a strategic point. If any invading army was able to take Harwich then they had a clear way to London. In 1667 the Dutch landed troops on the foreshore at Felixstowe and attempted to take Landguard Fort, but the Suffolk militia drove them away.

There was no town at Felixstowe when the Dutch came, the villages of Trimley and Walton were then the important places on the end of the Orwell-Deben Peninsula. The arrival of the railway, opened for passengers in 1855, made large-scale tourism possible. The new Victorian town of Felixstowe promoted itself by saying it had the only south-facing beach on the coast of Suffolk. The new resort went up market with some grand hotels on the sea front. When the Felix Hotel was opened in 1905 with fifty-two bedrooms it claimed to be the finest hotel on the East Coast. The rich and famous came to Felixstowe until 1939, but after World War II the resort was very popular with local people who had not been allowed near the sea during the war. The Felix Hotel was sold in 1952 and became Harvest House, the head office for the Ipswich firm of Fisons but in 1986 it was converted to flats.

The Port of Felixstowe grew on the cattle-grazing marshes beside the Harwich Harbour from a tiny Victorian dock in the 1950s, to one of the world's major container ports by the 1980s. In 2008 the hard facts about the Port of Felixstowe were that some 5,000 ships discharged containers here every year, involving fifty-five shipping companies with links to 365 ports around the world. This gave direct employment to 2,900 people and around 12,000 people working in associated industries. Although Felixstowe is of national importance it is also the reason why this corner of Suffolk formed a golden triangle of prosperity, with Ipswich and Woodbridge. In the 1980s more new buildings were put up in this triangle than in any other part of the British Isles.

The town of Felixstowe seems to have

Edwardian shelters beside the Sea Road, Felixstowe.

almost totally ignored the great port lying on the low land on its southern side. When London, Bristol and Liverpool became major ports they built prestige buildings, but Hamilton Road in Felixstowe has not altered much since the first Victorian summer visitors were driven from the station down to the cliff-top hotels. Felixstowe is a busy, but pleasant, unassuming town. The port has spawned a new hobby, ship-spotting. Down on Landguard Point there is a Viewing Area where men gather to recognize and record the huge variety of ships continually coming in to Felixstowe, Ipswich, Harwich and a few up the Stour to Mistley.

WOODBRIDGE

As the Woodbridge street system was impractical for road traffic it was decided to construct a major by-pass in about 1930 that is now part of the A12. This took the heavy road traffic away from the town centre and left the town as a backwater.

When I grew up in the 1940s no one ever said Woodbridge was beautiful, but by the 1980s the town was appearing in magazine as being one of East Anglia's most picturesque towns. The attractive Georgian houses in the town had long attracted genteel residents but Woodbridge changed, somewhere along the line, from being a working town to a highly desirable residential centre. There was no magic date when this took place. In the 1960s Woodbridge still had manufacturing firms giving employment and it was normal to park a car in the Thoroughfare at any time. Much of the town's prosperity revolved around the shops retailing goods to town and country people. In the 1960s the small light industries started to close, or in the case of Girdlestone's moved

A conker match was held at Felixstowe Ferry Sailing Club. Here, Robert Wright, commodore, is seen taking part. The winner was a 'sixty-fourer' conker.

The barges *May*, *Melissa* and *Dawn* at the 'Butt & Oyster ,' Pin Mill, 2009.

Ferryman John Barber, on the *Deben Ferry*, in 2008 making a sign to show that it was the last ferry of the season, between Bawdsey and Felixstowe.

to Melton, but by 1970 the town had shifted toward being a residential centre and pleasant place to visit.

By 2008 the Thoroughfare had been closed to daytime traffic and on a Saturday most of the town's parking places were full. Traffic and parking had become a real problem. Yet physically the main part of the town changed very little, apart from housing estates which have sprung up all around the town. The main change is that the whole area has become more affluent and far more crowded.

This subtle change is reflected in the shops. There had been family businesses retailing essential daily supplies and these have been replaced by shops selling luxury goods. This pattern was well under way when the first bookshop was opened in 1967. The shops are quite small, keeping the major chain stores away because they require large premises. However Woodbridge's population began to grow rapidly

in size and purchasing power. People saw opportunities to start new ventures and sought leases on the shops in the town. This demand pushed up the rents and many retail businesses did not last very long. After 2000 chain stores began to move into the Thoroughfare when much larger business premises were built.

ORFORD

If you go into a pub in Orford wearing walking boots, and carrying an Ordnance Survey map and a rucksack you will be considered perfectly normal. You will also be welcome because this town depends for its income on visitors who go walking, bird watching and on boat trips. Yet the local people, who mostly still speak in 'proper Suffolk', seldom know where the footpaths go or get on the river. They are too busy working hard to make a living from visitors to actually spend time walking around looking at the flat marshland.

Orford's first golden age was in the medieval period when it was a successful fishing port and the huge St Bartholomew Church was built. The town became a Borough in 1579, but when the mouth of the River Ore moved further to the south Orford declined as a fishing port. However the town continued to send two members to Parliament until it was classified as a 'Rotten Borough' and they were removed. Orford lost its status as a Borough in 1883, but the Orford Town Trust retained ownership of the River Ore.

Orford became the estate village for the Marquis of Hertford's great Sudbourne Hall Estate. By the 1920s the red brick houses were attracting private residents. In the 1940s Richard Pinney rented Ferry Cottage at Gedgrave and started to revive the oyster cultivation and to smoke fish. To find an outlet for their oysters Richard and Mathilde Pinney opened a shop on Orford's tiny market square and extended this into a fish restaurant. In the 1960s the London papers, searching for copy in rural England, were delighted to find a fish restaurant on the Suffolk coast. Reviewers were thrilled by Pinney's Butley-Orford Oysterage's lack of pretension, and it attracted visitors. Fifty years later Suffolk has hundreds of good eating-places but Orford has still retained a reputation for good food. At a time in 2008 when the 'Elephant & Castle' closed at Eyke due to lack of business the annual turnover of one of the pubs serving food in Orford was claimed to be over a million pounds a year. In the summer Orford also has a parking problem, which does not please some of the new residents.

Richard Pinney's son William has carried on with this progressive attitude to inshore fishing. In the 1970's William's *Julie EM*, a flat-bottomed high-speed craft, was the first 'fast-fisher' on the Suffolk coast. With this dory he could travel the long distance out to sea faster than the wooden clinker beach boats that were still being built for Aldeburgh fishermen. The high-speed craft cut down the time travelling to the open sea and this led to another powerful catamaran *Jolene*, based at Gedgrave Cliff on the Butley River. In 2007 *Jolene* was the most advanced fishing boat on the Sunrise Coast that worked all over the southern North Sea.

Other local men saw the potential in this new breed of fibreglass high-speed craft and Orford revived as a fishing centre. In 1994 there were five fast-fishers, some capable of twenty-four knots, working full time from Orford. In 2009 there were some part time fishing boats and the full time boats were *Girl Fiona* and Pete Benstead's *Faithful Star*, which supplies the small fresh fish shop on the river wall.

Orford still has its independent butcher's shop, which just about every town and village once had. Once, when talking to a lady in the butchers, who had moved down here from Islington, she remarked that Orford was a lovely place 'but one spends so much time going to the funerals of dear friends.' Orford, once a proud port and fishing town, had become a retirement and second homes centre.

There are two Orfords consisting of the Suffolk people and the new residents and they usually get on fine, but the two different ways of running thing clashed when Ralph Brinkley was sacked as harbour master. Ralph, whose family had long associations with the Orford River, looked on his job as harbour master as being his private fiefdom. However there was a great outcry and Ralph was reinstated as harbour master. When Ralph died in 2008 he received the highest honour the river front could give him; his photograph was hung up in the 'Jolly Sailor' along with other river worthies of the past, including his father Victor.

ALDEBURGH

Aldeburgh is pronounced 'Aldebro,' as it used to be spelt. In 2008 the *Sunday Times* called Aldeburgh 'the Suffolk Riviera,' but not because of its climate, that's for sure, but because of the up-market house prices and restaurants. The poet George Crabbe would have been amazed

The barge *Victor* at Maritime Woodbridge, 2008, The last barge to bring a cargo to Wodbridge was the *Edith May*, skippered by Jack Howard, son of the man who had the barge built in 1906.

that his hometown was ever being described in such flattering terms. When he had grown up here, in the late eighteenth century, Aldeburgh was a struggling port and fishing centre, chiefly noted for its poverty. It was, like the rest of the Suffolk coast, under siege from the North Sea. Crabbe was there in 1779 when huge waves came roaring in and washed eleven houses away. In 1783 he wrote about the town's squalid parish workhouse and Crabbe saw Aldeburgh as being a good place to leave. The effects of erosion and poverty drove him and many other people away. Later Crabbe wrote a grim poem, 'The Borough,' about a fisherman who beat and brutally mistreated his young apprentices. Storytellers never underestimate a situation, but Crabbe did appear to be referring to a real incident.

When the railways extended into East Anglia the trippers from The Midlands claimed the golden sands of Great Yarmouth and the north Norfolk coast, leaving the shingle beaches of Suffolk to the middle class families who could not afford the high prices of the South Coast hotels.

All this turned Aldeburgh into a unique and lovely place, but the sea breaking on the shingle beach has taken the heart out of the place. The centre of town should be grouped around the Moot Hall, but two streets have gone seaward. The successful defences carried out just after World War II saved the rest of the old town.

The red roofed part of Old Aldeburgh stretches like a ribbon along the beach and on the cliff top there are many fine houses. Aldeburgh thrives from its visiting population. It has some of the best hotels on the coast and in 2009, surprisingly, twenty-two clothes shops.

Plum Tree Cottage, Sudbourne being thatched, 2009. The Sandlings houses built in the late eighteenth and early nineteenth century had the local style of 'eye lid' windows and door tops. On the tiled rooves there are often brick ridges replacing bargeboards on the ends, and sometimes a row of projecting bricks below the roof eaves.

The Craft Shop in Front Street, Orford was a purpose-built coach house. The mail coach left at 9am in the morning for Woodbridge, Felixstowe and Ipswich.

The Pugh's bathing machine on the sea front at Aldeburgh, 2008. The bathing machines were on Aldeburgh beach by 1860 and had four wheels so that they could be pushed down to the water's edge for ladies to enter the sea, with the help of modesty screens. Aldeburgh was the one Suffolk resort that didn't have beach huts, but after World War II some bathing machines remained as changing rooms.

Wood's fish stand on the Crag Path, Aldeburgh. The Aldeburgh inshore fishing boats survived because they could retail the fish landed straight to the public.

There were some 'bait sheds' on the beach where fishermen could bait their longlines for cod, but most fishermen stored their gear in their cottages. As the new residents moved in, mostly after the 1953 floods, the fishermen put up sheds near the Moot Hall. In 2008 there were still fourteen sheds on the beach, although only six fishermen were working, where there had once been sixty. Some people bought boats so that they could have a shed on the beach for storage or holiday homes. In 2008 a meeting was held, with more than the number at a meeting about Sizewell C, and it was agreed that only fishermen should use the sheds.

At the height of the summer Aldeburgh is heaving with people, and it is difficult to park, but for much of the year, when the second homeowners and visitors go away, the place is unnaturally quiet.

The popularity of Aldeburgh, at least in part, is due to Crabbe's poem which Suffolk composer Benjamin Britten turned into the opera 'Peter Grimes.' This was first performed at Sadlers Wells in 1945, and was a tremendous success. Britten and his partner, the singer Peter Pears, and the librettist Eric Crozior went to a music festival at Lucerne and thought the idea of a Music Festival could be adapted to Suffolk. Aldeburgh welcomed the idea, as the town needed a few more tourists in the summer. The first Aldeburgh Festival was held in 1948 and grew in size and influence after Britten and Pears settled in the town. Although Aldeburgh Festival has always been primarily devoted to music, particularly Britten's, it has extended to other arts.

The original Aldeburgh Festival was very exclusive and revolved around a small tightly knit group of people, but in time it opened out. Estate agents claimed that they could relate the rise in property prices in Aldeburgh to the steady growth of the Aldeburgh Festival. Originally the concerts were held in the Jubilee Hall and churches in the district and a major step forward was the creation of the first concern hall at Snape Maltings in 1967. Aldeburgh Music has developed an all year programme and has grown in importance and local political power. The Snape complex steadily expanded to include a music school, and in 2009 another concert hall was opened.

The people of Aldeburgh care about its appearance, although passions can run deep on how that is to be achieved. The town roughly splits up into four groups: the weekenders mainly from Greater London, the retired population, local business people who just want more visitors and the local Suffolk people who sometimes resent newcomers, but when they sell their houses they want the highest price they can get. Generally speaking the people who have come and settled in Aldeburgh are highly social, good mixers and brilliant organizers, but not wildly pleased to see all the visitors the town now attracts.

LEISTON

Leiston is not an ancient town and has few listed buildings, but it is kept neat and tidy by the people who enjoy living here. There is always a demand for accommodation in Leiston because of the changing work force at the Sizewell Power Station. Because of this rented accommodation it also attracts workers from Eastern Europe to settle here, mostly for the farm work and the building trade.

It only takes six minutes to travel by car from Aldeburgh to Leiston. The smart houses on the Warren fade out at the Hundred River. Aldringham is briefly rural and then the road leads to the terraced houses of Leiston. Aldeburgh has culture and expensive houses and Leiston has an industrial heritage. The two places are totally different.

In the medieval period Sizewell was the dominant market town on the coast, but the sea washed it away. Leiston Abbey was originally near the coast, but erosion and flooding forced the Abbey to relocate inland. Leiston was just a village until the Garrett family started an iron foundry here in 1778. As the farms were trying to push up food production and cut down labour costs there was a tremendous demand for the farm machinery. Garrett's machines cut down the drudgery of rural life and by the Victorian era their products were being exported to the Empire. In 1900 Garretts engineering works employed over a thousand people and couldn't keep up with the worldwide demand for its steam engines. Leiston was a nineteenth century industrial town set in amongst the green fields of rural Suffolk.

Garretts of Leiston, like many nineteenth century industrial firms, died slowly and finally closed its doors in 1980. Garrett's Long

Iken Cliff with the barge yacht *Hawthorn* on her mooring. The granary and coal store at Iken Cliff was used to supply coal etc. to the Saxmundham area until the flat bottom sailing barges made it easier to take freights further up to Snape.

Ron Geater with plants at L.F.Geater & Sons Ltd, West End Nurseries, Leiston. Geaters have about four acres 'under glass' and employ about twenty-five people producing cut flowers for the national wholesale market.

Shop, opened in 1855, is a unique nineteenth century industrial building. An assembly line for building steam engines built eighty years before Henry Ford pushed the idea forward for cars in the United States. After Garretts closed the main factory area, near the railway station, was slowly redeveloped, but fortunately its importance was recognized in the town and in 1983 the Long Shop was opened as a museum.

Aldeburgh dealt with the decline of the fishing industry by opening art galleries and restaurants. Leiston didn't have the sea to attract tourists and unemployment was becoming a problem in this rural corner of Suffolk. The building of Sizewell A nuclear power station in 1961-6 was popular in the town because its construction brought in much-needed employment. The building of the second nuclear power station, Sizewell B, sparked off a national debate and strong opposition, but again Sizewell welcomed the employment it created.

Before the second nuclear power station was built at Sizewell there was the longest running public enquiry in British history. The enquiry started in 1983 at Snape Concert Hall and went on for two years. Everyone saw the danger, but no-one wanted the lights to go out because there was not enough electricity and Sizewell B Power station was built between 1991-6.

SAXMUNDHAM

'Sax' has a sense of community and people enjoy living there, but for most people it is just a town they pass through on the way to somewhere else. The towns heyday was probably when the stage-coaches ran through here. The 'Bell' was built in 1842 and was one of the last of the great coaching inns. It was one of the stops of the 'Old Blue' coach, running to Great Yarmouth, but the railway arrived on the same route in a few years and killed the stage-coaches overnight. The centre of Saxmundham has never quite recovered its former glory.

Saxmundham is a reminder of Woodbridge in the 1940s, it relies on local people from the villages coming in to do their shopping. Although the A12 was diverted around the town there is still a great deal of traffic along the High Street. In fact, because it is a narrow street it feels dangerous to walk along it and this puts visitors off coming to shop in the town.

Lady Caroline Cranbrook, and other campaigners, fought a planning battle to prevent Tesco from building a superstore beside the A12 road. It was argued that if a superstore opened on the A12 it would drag all the trade away from the local shops. Local food producers largely supplied the small shops, in the Thoroughfare, and their loss would seriously damage the local economy. Because of the success of this campaign 'Sax' has retained the feeling of being a genuine small country town.

WALBERSWICK

Walberswick is a 'rags to riches' story. When Dunwich harbour was washed away the trade and fishing moved to Southwold harbour, but the shingle bar frequently closed its mouth. Ashore life of the fisherfolk of Walberswick in the nineteenth century was lived on the edge of poverty. If that was not bad enough some of the local smacks were lost at sea. In 1883 the Walberswick smack *Clipper* was lost in the North Sea with all nine men aboard. The *Clipper's* owner Robert English and two of his sons went down with the smack. Robert's wife Lydia lived on to be over ninety, she died in 1927, and because she could read and write, used to draw up people's wills.

One of Robert English's surviving sons, Tom English, saw the way forward was to cater for summer visitors. In 1910 he built the Harbour View. The front half of the house was let out to visitors in the summer and the family went up through a trap door to sleep at the back. In 1990 I spoke with Leslie Goodwin,

great-grandson of Robert English, and his wife Ruth at the Harbour View. Ruth, chairman of the Parish Council at the time, observed that very few local people who were born and bred in the village could now afford to buy a house there. The price of houses in Walberswick was a third higher than similar houses the other side of the main A12 road. Ruth Goodwin joked that Walberswick should be renamed 'Little Hampstead by the Sea.'

Down beside the harbour on the Flats, where fishermen used to a have a big copper for boiling cotton nets to preserve them, there is a large car park for visitors. Many of the fishermen's sheds down near the Harbour were removed in 1938, during one of the many harbour improvement schemes, but the red brick Granary and others were converted to holiday homes.

It was Walberswick's quirky ramshackle character that attracted artists here in the late nineteenth century, along with the fact that accommodation was cheaper here than in the fashionable resorts. The painter Philip Wilson Steer came here for several summers from 1884, while the Scottish Art Nouveau architect Charles Rennie Mackintosh lived here from 1914 to 1915. Walberswick attracts famous names, but they seem to stay out of sight.

Walberswick, in the medieval period, centred around the church and from here Stocks Lane leads down to the Westwood Marshes, the largest reed bed in the United Kingdom. The bottom of Stocks Lane is where Walberswick had a quay on the Dunwich River and a shipbuilding yard. The largest ship built here was the 28 gun *HMS Baring* in 1654 but they had great difficulty in getting her down the Dunwich River into Southwold Harbour.

The Westwood Marshes were drained in the eighteenth century and in 1897 a brick pump windmill was built to pump water into the former Dunwich River. An iron wheel, with wooden paddles, lifted up the water. A marshman, who looked after the horses, cattle and sheep on the marshes, also worked the

In 1997 the 248 beach huts at Southwold became known nationally because they started to change hands for very high prices. Over the next decade their value became about a third of the price of some small houses.